THE AWAKENED WARRIOR TOOLKIT

EMPOWERING STORIES AND SPIRITUAL TOOLS TO
SUPPORT YOUR AWAKENING JOURNEY IN
TRANSFORMING LIFE'S CHALLENGES INTO COURAGE
AND CONFIDENCE.

CAROL ANN REID

AND CO.

DISCLAIMER

In parts throughout this book, the co-authors may describe events, locales and conversations from their memories. Sometimes, in order to maintain their anonymity, in some instances we have changed the names of individuals and places, we may have changed some identifying characteristics and details such as physical properties, occupations and places of residence.

Although the co-authors and publisher have made every effort to ensure that the information in this book was correct at press time, the co-authors and publisher do not assume and hereby disclaim any liability to any party for any loss, damage, or disruption caused by errors or omissions, whether such errors or omissions result from negligence, accident, or any other cause.

CONTENTS

1

FREE THE WARRIOR WITHIN AND SHE WILL LIGHT THE WAY

CAROL-ANN REID

Just as we have transformed and transitioned from the industrial age to present times, known as the information age, we are currently at the dawn of yet another evolutionary transformation and transition; the intuitive age.

The industrial age saw an awakening of our physical abilities as humans, with masculine energy being the prominent driving force. During this time, we were forced to live our lives in alignment with our physical abilities and identity. Women cooked and looked after children, children were seen and not heard, and men made a living through heavy labour to provide for the family.

Humans have evolved alongside technology, we've lived in an information and consumer-driven world for the past few decades; an existence that has advanced us in numerous ways, yet simultaneously paralysed us. We are no longer required to leave the house to see loved ones on the other side of the world, ready-made meals can be delivered to us with the touch of a few buttons, money is rapidly turning digital, and an answer to any question can be found online in a matter of seconds.

We have the world at our fingertips, yet here we are in an age of crisis, with eyes glued to screens, physical connection at an all-time low and mental health problems fast becoming the next pandemic. Bombarded with information from all directions, our logical brains are on overload. Many people feel like they have just as many browser tabs open in their minds, as they do on their computers.

But as human beings, we are more than just our physical and mental selves. We are each a unique, magnificent cocktail of energy and emotions, each harbouring a spiritual self. At a core level, we are driven by our emotions and feelings.

But many have fallen into the well of allowing the logical, analytical side of the brain to run the show, often referred to as left-brained thinking. In minimising the use of the right side of the brain, our intuitive senses, imagery, and creativity get stumped. You may hear some people call this 'woo-woo' or airy-fairy talk, but it is not to be underestimated, as it plays an incredibly important role in our emotional intelligence and awakenings.

In this lightning-paced world, people are burying their emotions, differences, identity, and intuition in an attempt to fit in, often turning to escapism if it all feels too much. The result? Our sense of self is becoming lost in the sea of illusion. Information and perceived perfection leave us feeling not enough, and a strong need to be liked and accepted becomes the goal.

I, too, fell into this deep, dark well. The need for acceptance from others controlled me, the fear of judgment halted my every move and often, doubt smothered my intuition. Like many of the fellow Warriors in this book have experienced, this led to trauma, pain, and crumbling self-confidence.

But a new age is on the horizon, and you will find yourself amongst it on the pages of these chapters. I, and the nine other incredible authors, invite you to journey with us into this future with an open mind, a valiant heart, and a child-like curiosity.

Because curiosity never did kill the cat.

The belief in that tale killed curiosity.

THE NEW AGE WE ARE FAST APPROACHING IS THE 'INTUITIVE AGE'.

Children are born embodying a free spirit. Look around a playground to see boundless energy and limitless imagination as sticks transform into space rockets, teddies become afternoon tea-loving picnic goers, and trees represent hideouts from pirates. Confidence and self-belief are part of the package of being a kid; intuition and imagination guide their every move.

But as we grow, so does an expectation to conform. Speak when spoken to, wear a uniform, listen, and accept everything you are taught. Generations of conditioning are passed down through our parents and caregivers (unbeknown to them) until eventually, our unique lights are extinguished and the intuitive flame flickers out.

Like the death of a star, we don't realise that the light has gone out until many years later.

During my training to become a Master Timeline Therapist and Hypnotherapist, a memory surfaced that had been buried as a young child. Around the age of six, our primary school announced they were putting on a whole school play of Cinderella. I was ecstatic when the teachers announced my name as Cinderella. A couple of my best friends were cast as the 'ugly sisters' (what even was Disney back then?!) but either way, we were all so supportive of each other and excited that we had lines to say!

I recalled a memory of seeing one of my best friends' mums ask our teacher in a very passive-aggressive way, "why did *she* get the role of Cinderella and not my daughter?" I am unable to provide the answer the teacher gave; my mind and body were too busy imprinting that poisonous question of "why her?". I'm sure the parent never intended for me to hear her, but I did.

For over twenty-five years, I carried that question around with me subconsciously in everything I did. "Why me?" Why am I worthy of a lead role? Transitioning into adulthood, the question altered into why am I worthy of loving relationships? Why am I good enough to get that job? Who am I to grow my own successful business? When I started achieving success, I put it down to luck or downplayed it. Over the years, a deep need to stay feeling safe from judgment led to me over-giving, feeling the need to overachieve, and never accepting that I had done enough to warrant success or fulfilment.

I've seen this pattern occur repeatedly with the men and women I've worked with in coaching and healing. You yourself, or someone you know, *is* or has struggled with the aftermath of trauma. Trauma is complex and exists in many forms, affecting everyone differently. I like to recognise it as experiencing trauma with a big T, or little t. This is as individual to us as our unique fingerprints.

Not all trauma involves near-death experiences, abuse, or immediately life-threatening events. For many, just like my own personal example, our experiences of trauma are with a little t and often go unnoticed, unspoken about, or you get told "you'll get over it" because it's not a huge deal at the time. A teacher embarrassed you in front of your classmates, you got picked last on the sports team, you forgot to pack your knickers on the school swimming day (speaking from experience here!), your parents were different to others, you couldn't afford the cool school shoes.

An event that impacts you emotionally, physically, mentally, or spiritually as a child or adult, can leave a lasting imprint within you, as your nervous system explodes like a firework, leaving an energetic signature from that event. This is where fears reside, causing unconscious fears of failure, judgment, shame, and a burning need to stay safe. Safe from physical harm, but also emotional and mental distress. We become creatures of habit and comfort.

We each journey through our own experiences, trauma, and struggles in life, but awakening to the knowing that it does not define you, nor does it have to hold you back, can awaken new layers of self-belief and acceptance.

Love, confidence, abundance, fulfilment, and joy *is* your birthright.

Often, our unique life experiences and conditionings cause us to put up protective barriers around our hearts and detach from our authentic selves, and our ultimate life paths. Learning to trust in yourself just enough to suspend your beliefs and open your mind and heart to a new way of being and living, is nothing short of transformational.

I urge you to hold space to recognise that any pain from your past can be your greatest superpower when you begin your journey of acceptance and healing. This is a part of awakening to your aligned, authentic self. And when you are your authentic self, you wake up craving adventure and joy and see the world through a whole new lens.

Throughout my adult life, I've experienced the loss of a loved one to suicide, been at the bedside of my best friend after she took her last breath, I've experienced traumatic relationships, and lost my business and my way in life.

I now believe that a huge part of our awakening and divine plan is to journey, heart first, through the highest of highs and lowest of lows of life; trusting that even when we are walking painful paths or feeling out of control, somehow, someway, it will all work out for the best.

A part of this process is learning to tune out from the outside noise and tune in to our internal, intuitive selves, dropping from our logical, information-fuelled minds, into our hearts and intuitive self. After all, the Latin meaning of intuition is inner-tutor.

In my career as a transformational life coach and business mindset mentor, I've witnessed these transformative awakenings over and over again - the moment people learn it's safe to drop from their heads into their hearts. That they can, in fact, strengthen their connection to their intuition and become their own guiding light.

It's the experiences we go through in life that ultimately gift us our awakening moments.

What we go through, we grow through.

YOUR MESS IS YOUR MESSAGE.

At the time, whilst in the depths of what can feel like hell, it is almost impossible to comprehend how the experiences could one day be a moment you'll reflect on and think "I now understand why that had to happen".

You may find it within yourself to make peace with your past and accept yourself. For many, you will even find gratitude for those messy moments, realising that despite it all, you're still here.

This book shares real-world stories from courageous warrior women who maybe, just like you, couldn't see a way out at times. For most, they reached breaking point, feeling like the world was crashing down around them, that they didn't belong, and that something just *had* to change in their lives.

Little did they know at the time, that it was these Divine moments that triggered awakening impulses, that ruptured through their lives and souls. The burning desire or desperation for change churned up an energy like no other. It's this tenacious hope and courageous grit that plays a significant role in their awakenings. Something within them awoke that had once lay dormant, as they now realised that their biggest breakdowns were their greatest breakthroughs.

Just like excavating a precious jewel, you must dig deep to uncover the beautiful treasure.

I invite you, throughout this book, to pause and reflect on your own experiences. Borrow our confidence and courage to reflect on your own life, through the lens of a warrior.

What if you too have been through moments of awakening? Imagine those chapters in your life that ground you to a halt, unlocking a greater conscious awareness and growing ability to shift your perception (with practice) from 'why me' to 'I see'.

Awakenings, whether you classify them as spiritual or not, are cracks that allow your inner light to beam through from the inside out. Choosing to look through your warrior lens will help you understand that when attentively healed, loved, and nurtured, your battle wounds will form scar tissue, which is stronger than regular skin.

In time, you can then begin to shed that old skin. Just like a caterpillar evolves into a chrysalis, within its protective casing, the caterpillar radically transforms its entirety, eventually emerging as a butterfly.

You may not have realised that you too are, in fact, walking the warrior path of awakening; your hidden jewels waiting to be uncovered. The dream career isn't only for others to experience, healthy relationships aren't just for the 'lucky' ones, and wealth and abundance aren't only available for a certain kind of person.

What if this book has come to you at just the right time? *The Divine time.*

Now, I know what you may be thinking: how can it be 'Divine timing' when you made a conscious decision to buy it from Amazon or were gifted it by a friend? Sharing another personal awakening journey may inspire hope within you and 'myth bust' what so often gets put down to 'coincidence'.

After spending most of my twenties trying to satisfy a deep inner need for belonging and feeling enough, I finally abandoned the drugs, dangerous men and fake friends, leaving the party lifestyle and travel (i.e., escapism) behind.

It took me arriving at a physical breaking point to make that decision, but the night I escaped my old life and drove home in the early hours, weak and delirious after being held captive for two days, was an awakening moment I'll never forget.

My spiritual awakening has supported me in accepting what happened and forgiving (not forgetting) him and myself, not because I think what happened was right - far from it - but because my inner peace is my priority.

Here's the thing with healing; the old advice of 'forgive and forget' or 'just let it go' holds no weight. You don't forget the experiences you go through, and you don't always have to forgive them either – acceptance can be just as powerful, if not more. Healing through coaching or therapy doesn't erase what you went through, but instead enables you to process the trauma on all levels: mentally, emotionally, physically, and the one that often gets overlooked, spiritually. Recalibrating your nervous system; freeing you from the body's holographic memories that frequently get triggered unconsciously.

Before healing and awakening from this experience, certain songs, smells, even names, would trigger the fight, flight, freeze, or fawn trauma responses within me. I recall having coffee with a friend around a year after the event, when a song came on the radio while we were catching up. An instant tidal wave of adrenaline and fear took over my body causing me to shake and tear up, and the overwhelming need to escape paralysed me. This was the nervous system's imprint signalling to my body IT'S NOT SAFE, GET OUT. Yet it was only a song, and consciously, I knew I was safe.

Past pain can feel like you're carrying around a ten-tonne skeleton on your back. Along with the burden of that weight comes the fear that others may one day discover the bones of your past; judging and shaming you for them.

But if you were to look at yourself in a mirror, deep into your eyes, and see past the trauma, mistakes, 'what ifs', or regrets, you'll begin to see yourself for who you *truly* are. You'll see an inner child looking for comfort, love, and adventure. You'll see a strong as hell warrior who, despite everything, has made it through to today. You'll see wisdom, energy, source, and spirit. Because that is the true essence of who you are.

I lugged heavy bones around on my back for over a decade. Since letting the skeletons out of my closet and committing to the healing work, I've fully accepted my past and the person it has enabled me to become. I have *finally* given myself permission to be my unedited, unfiltered self and, WOW, is this awakening freeing!

It is safe for you to be loved. It's safe to let your authentic light shine, and if your brightness hurts other people's eyes, know that it's safe to pass them some shades and keep being you.

My awakening moments have led me to meet my husband Karl, manifest our first dream home, discover my calling of being a transformational life coach and mindset expert, growing a successful brand, become an author and speaker, bringing our beautiful twin boys, Blake and Carter, into the world after fertility issues, connecting to spirit and believing in the power of the universe, and even angels! Rewind to six years ago, when I was asked if I believe in angels and guides, it was a firm no! But never say never.

I now feel more connected to a deeper purpose in life; all of the above presented itself during a time that felt like I was going off the beaten track and having no idea how to get back on. When you go within for answers, your intuition lights up like an oil lamp. There is a need to lean in closely and nurture the flickering flame, combined with trusting that you may only be able to see one step ahead of you at a time. That one crucial step is taking you forward on your path.

ASK AND YOU SHALL RECEIVE.

After the loss of a loved one to suicide and my best friend to cancer, my career and life ground to a halt. Something within kept telling me to do the inner work and be vulnerable for a change. My own healing journey became a catalyst for me re-training and transitioning my career into what it is today.

My coaching practice began growing quickly, and I finally felt in alignment. I remember the moment I was sitting at my dining room table when, like a lightning bolt, an idea for a product-based business came to me. I was overwhelmed with excitement as I got clarity on the name, the process, the purpose and mission. It felt magical, like it had been downloaded into me.

I excitedly shared the idea with someone I had met around six months prior, they were very successful, oozed confidence and had a level of unshakable self-belief that I had never witnessed before.

After sharing a Dragon's Den style pitch, they jumped onboard, and we began our venture together. However, I felt like I was a 5-year-old kid wearing my mum's shoes. There was a niggle within me that I couldn't put my finger on, nor could I shift. But I insisted on telling myself that the anxiety I was feeling was just excitement.

As the months rolled by, I ignored the red flags. I was shrinking myself down in fear of doing or saying anything wrong. Old wounds surfaced and I began struggling with stuttering and IBS, as old patterns with food emerged. I found myself binge eating and calorie controlling again as my anxiety reached a height I hadn't experienced before.

My intuition was screaming for my attention; warning me things must change. However, I felt trapped, deeply convincing myself that it was all down to me. If I change then surely things will improve?

After almost two years of pushing my gut feelings to one side and muting the whispers from my intuition, I broke.

Holding my head in my hands, I sat at my desk in my home office. To the outside world, I painted on a smile and looked like I had the whole world at my feet yet, crying quietly, I picked up a picture that was nestled on my desk. It was a photo of me and my best friend Karen, who had passed away, enjoying dinner and one too many glasses of bubbly together. She had surprised me with a mini-cruise, and I fell in love with holidaying that way the moment we set foot on the ship together.

The happy memories came flooding back to me, but the pain of missing her words of wisdom floored me. The first piece of advice she gave me many moons ago was "Say yes, then learn how to do it after". I felt I had been honouring that advice, but it felt distorted, like I was floundering my way through a career and business I adored, but at the detriment to my mental and physical health.

In that moment, I placed my thumb onto her heart on the photograph and found myself whispering, "please help me?" As more tears tumbled down my cheeks, I begged her, "please guide me, I don't know what to do".

Aware of the business meeting I had the following day, I fell into bed with tired eyes, as knots formed in the pit of my stomach. Awakening the next morning, I tried shaking off the nerves with a shower and repeatedly declaring, "I am strong, I've got this", but affirmations weren't cutting the mustard.

Startled by my phone ringing, I glanced at it, quickly placing it back down on the side. A number I didn't recognise flashed on the screen, but I had zero energy for anything else in that moment. It continued ringing, as if whoever was calling knew that I was near my phone but refusing to pick up. After around the ninth or tenth ring, I answered with a sharp tone, "Hello?".

I didn't recognise the voice on the other end of the receiver. I could sense an accent, but it wasn't strong enough to pinpoint. She started by saying "I'll make this quick as I know you've got an important day ahead". Sorry? My towel dropped to the bedroom floor, now I was feeling even more vulnerable, but I continued listening.

This wise voice immediately started insisting that I go to the meeting today and stand my ground. She went on to demand that I not get swayed or taken off course and that Archangel Michael would watch over me. She ended by telling me to call her back on this number later, after my meeting.

My jaw dropped next to my towel on the floor. I scrambled for the right words; wanting to ask questions like who are you? How do you know? But intuitively, something inside of me screamed, just LISTEN.

The last words of that brief conversation ended with "Oh, and your friend is with you". Words I will never forget.

"Karen"? I asked through tears that instantaneously fell from my face. "Yes, she's with you".

"Thank you" I mumbled through the shock.

Without time to process, I got ready for that meeting in a head and heart space I had never been in before. I felt overwhelmed with confusion, but like I had an invisible army by my side. The meeting went as expected, but I stood in my power. We came face to face, and when I was asked a question about the future plans of the business and my intentions, I spoke with conviction and courage.

For the first time, I felt a wave of confidence flood through me. Yes, it was met with hostility but somehow, the belief that someone, or something greater than myself was by my side, helped me awaken my own strength.

My relationship with the lady who called me that morning grew, and I will forever refer to her as my earth angel guide. It turned out we had met a few months previous through a company I held weekly mindset workshops for. We had exchanged business cards and I recall thinking she made me feel at ease when I first met her, there was something about her that oozed calmness and trust.

We went on to exchange many calls over the coming months, as she held space for me to reflect and see the wood for the trees, whilst awakening a spiritual connection within me that had lay dormant for the entirety of my adult life.

It took me some time to ask how she knew to call that morning. *Was it a coincidence that I asked my friend's picture for help and guidance the night before? Was it pure luck?* Part of me was craving a logical explanation, yet another part of me enjoyed the wonder and curiosity. "I felt the calling" was the answer she calmly gave me.

Just as we all have daily fleeting thoughts; I had 'coincidently' crossed her mind on that exact evening. It just so happened to occur at the same time I had broken down in tears in my office, speaking to my friend I'd lost, praying for her to somehow support me.

She went on to explain her sudden thought about me and the first time we met, and as she did, she felt a strong desire to reach out to me. It felt like someone was telling her I needed her help. I later learnt that behind her very corporate front-facing job, she was someone who had lived with psychic abilities for many years.

My belief of what was possible for us humans cracked right open. It awakened an unshakable knowing that the abilities we have not only physically, but mentally, emotionally, and spiritually are limitless.

It also confirmed a knowing that the path I was on, simply wasn't right for me. Anxiety and shattered confidence weren't who I truly was. These were symptoms of something deeper, something more meaningful. My decision to walk away was a painful one, but the right one.

The evening we finalised it all, was the night before I was due to go on a family holiday with my husband, dad and brother. Adrenaline shot through my veins having done it, and I drove home in an anxiety-induced trance. Only when I got home did it register what I'd done. Followed by the second realisation that we were going to the airport in just nine hours!

Pouring myself a large glass of red, I went upstairs to attempt packing. Barely concentrating, I knocked my glass of wine over on my cream office carpet and I burst into tears. Not because it was an expensive wine or the carpet was stained, but because of the emptiness I felt. A trembling shadow of who I truly was.

Whilst knelt cleaning the wine and my salty tears out of the carpet, I glanced in the direction of my bookshelf. It looked like a giant blur of overwhelm, but something made me close my bloodshot eyes and run my finger along the spine of all the books.

As I opened my eyes, my finger was locked onto a book I had been given a year or so before. It originally belonged to Karen. A family friend had found it in her bedside drawer years after she passed over, and something made her pass it on to me.

I never felt called to read it back then, the title and gist of the book didn't resonate. Regardless, having something belonging to her meant the world to me, so I had kept it on my bookshelf. As I placed the book into my suitcase, I felt a small wave of calm wash over me.

A couple of days into the holiday, I was laid on a sun lounger staring out at sea, still trying to figure out logically, *now what?* Whilst doing my best to relax and enjoy the holiday we had all worked so hard for, I suddenly recalled part of an audio book I had listened to a few weeks prior, a Gabrielle Bernstein one where she talks about asking for a sign.

I desperately needed a sign. Staring out into the vast sea, I asked the universe "if I have made the right decision and this is a new path that's meant for me, please show me the sign of a… dragonfly".

I instantly questioned myself! A dragonfly?! On a cruise ship in the middle of the ocean? *"Let it go,"* said the inner voice. I grabbed my now melted strawberry daiquiri and took a sip.

My brother and husband came over around twenty minutes later and pleaded with me to come and try the rock climbing wall. Trying their hardest to lift my spirits and keep me strong, I agreed to watch. In my own little world, I smiled as I observed a couple of children abseil down a huge climbing wall, whilst thinking how wonderfully fearless we are at that age.

I recall the next moment in slow motion, because to me, it was like time had stood still. From behind me, my brother shouted *"quick, quick, come look... it's a dragonfly!"*. I paused, before slowly turning around. Did he know? How would he know?

A crowd had gathered around my brother as I brushed through the sticky, sun-creamed shoulders of those who were in awe of what they could see on the deck of the cruise ship. There it was, a shimmering blue, purple and turquoise dragonfly. I crouched down to get a closer look. My heart felt struck by the pure beauty of it as the colours caught the sunlight.

I took a breath, *"Thank you"* I whispered. In that moment, I felt the presence of the invisible spirit army around me once again. Like my caged, broken wings were being mended, and my hurt, heavy heart felt hope once again.

That simple, yet profound sign gave me enough hope to start reading the book that had been passed to me from Karen's bedside table. 'Manual of the Warrior of Light' by Paulo Coelho. I underlined nearly every word, re-reading sentences that felt like they had been written for my eyes only. How had this been sat on my bookshelf for over a year, and only NOW I'm reading it?

This was my first experience of understanding Divine timing. Reading it before then wouldn't have had the same impact. I was too deep in the trenches to have comprehended the messages. I was busy evolving, breaking out of the cocoon and sharpening my warrior sword of courage.

This is one of many examples of synchronicities and guidance from the universe that still, until this day, blows me away. Following my intuition has guided me to create the Awaken the Warrior community; coaching, talks, workshops, programs, membership, and of course, led to the Warrior toolkit collaboration books, alongside the incredible warrior women you are about to meet.

When I reflect on this chapter of my life, I do so through the Warrior lens. With unconditional gratitude and love. As hard as it was at the time, it's been a pivotal part of my awakening and spiritual growth. I send gratitude and light to those involved, as I now see that our life paths were meant to cross at that time, for the lessons to be lived and embodied.

SIGNS, SYMBOLS, AND COINCIDENCES.

'Coincidences' often get put down to luck, right place right time, flukes and one offs. Over time we have warped the meaning of a coincidence, diluting it to something much less than it is. I recall saying to myself that from now on, I'm going to replace the word coincidence with *synchronicity*. Thanking the universe, whilst trusting that it's all working itself out for the highest good of myself, and the highest good of all involved. The level of peace this gives you is beautiful.

I truly believe that if you have an open heart, what is meant for you will never pass you by.

What I choose to believe when I reflect over chapters in my life:

- Had I not lost a loved one to suicide, I wouldn't have had the drive and courage to transition my career into coaching.
- Had I not fallen into drugs and lost myself, I wouldn't have gone on a quest to discover myself.
- Had I not asked for a sign; I would have remained in my head, questioning myself and my choices.
- Had I not trusted the process and read that book, I wouldn't have resonated with the Warrior of Light and found the strength to start my business over from scratch.

As you'll discover in the rest of the book, these golden threads run strongly through all these Warrior Women. My guess is if you were drawn to this book, you too have a Warrior awakening within you.

Reflecting on your life and all you've been through, our hope is that you see a piece of yourself weaved throughout the empowering stories shared. Take the tools and guidance that resonate with you, so you too can feel a new level of strength and courage rise from within you.

Remember, awakening is unique to us all, and there's no ending to it. No certificate to say you've passed or fanfare to welcome you to the higher realms of alignment, manifestation, and happiness. Just an undeniable knowing that you are more than what meets the eye, and powerful beyond measure. There is a tribe of Warriors just like yourself, ready to march side by side on similar journeys.

Awakening and healing doesn't have to be a lonely journey. When you choose to surround yourself with like-minded and like-hearted people, your growth and confidence soars. When you invest in yourself and surrender to professional support and guidance, your healing quantum leaps. The wounds that were too deep to see within yourself evolve and transpire into purpose, clarity, and inner peace.

Teaching and working with thousands of Warrior men and women in the last half decade, I can say with unshakeble belief that *anything* in this life is possible for you.

Here are some of the tools that I regularly use and recommend supporting your awakening journey, to cultivate harmony between your mental, spiritual, and emotional self:

Meditation – whether it's five minutes of sitting in silence whilst focusing on your breathing, a walking meditation, or listening to a guided recording that takes you on an inner journey. Meditation is a practice that once you start and feel the benefits, you will never go without!

Affirmation, angel, and oracle cards – Affirmation cards are a great starting place, then angel, oracle and tarot are incredible for deeper connection to self, source and spirit. Try pulling a daily card for either guidance or inspiration for 21 days, you'll soon begin to see the synchronicities taking place within you, and around you.

Ask better questions – replace the "why me" and "what if" questions with "what could this be teaching me?" "What am I not seeing that could help support me through this?" "What advice would my intuition or higher self give me?" "If I was to trust deeper, what would that look like?" You hold the greatest wisdom within you, start to really trust this voice.

See the world through child-like eyes – When you stop taking yourself and life so seriously, old conditioning begins to fall away. Focus on less judgment and more laughter, less worry and more play, less fear and more acceptance, less doubt and more courage.

A reason, a season, or a lifetime – friendships and relationships come and go throughout life. When you awaken and begin living your life in full alignment, you may find that some cheer you on, whilst others run. This isn't about you, it's that you are mirroring back to them parts of themselves yet to be healed or awakened, causing them to question their path, growth and worth. If you find yourself reflecting on a friendship or relationship, trust your heart and gut with what category they entered your life. Ask yourself; was it for a reason, a season or a lifetime? Then act accordingly.

Gratitude is medicine for the mind – Gratitude helps ground you in the present moment as you recognise all the blessings you already have in your life. Gratitude practices help soothe your nervous system and enhance your mood as your brain releases dopamine and serotonin, the two 'feel good' chemicals.

Try using my 3,2,1 Gratitude Method, you can write these down daily, or think them to yourself:

- 3 things you're grateful for in life
- 2 people you're grateful for in life
- 1 thing you're grateful for, that's on its way to you

Follow the signs, synchronicities, and symbols. Some people see white feathers or ask for specific signs. Others begin seeing repeated numbers such as 111 or 22.22 on the clock, often referred to as angel numbers. If your curiosity feels lit up, follow the calling, and trust your own interpretation of what you are seeing or sensing.

May this book awaken more of your own authentic light and free the buried treasure within you. The courage you need is within you now, I offer my hand and heart to you on this journey. May our paths cross, and one day, I hope to read your own story of awakening.

MY FIVE KEY TAKEAWAYS

1. We are moving from the information age into the intuitive age. This transition will shake up and challenge many of the systems and conditionings we live amongst. Stay true to you and trust the process.

2. We each experience trauma in life, whether that's with a big T, or little t. Your experiences and emotions matter, no matter how it was handled at the time. It's never too late to heal and grow.

3. Ask for specific signs and trust. If you receive your sign, take it for what it is (you don't need to ask again to double check!) and trust that you're being guided.

4. It's okay not to have it all figured out. Sometimes things must fall apart, in order to piece back together in a way your logical mind could never have comprehended.

5. Find your awakened tribe and love them hard. When you come across "your people", those you resonate with and feel at home with, let them see and feel you for all that you are. You'll find such a unique love and flow with those who are on the same wavelength as you.

Dedication

I dedicate this chapter to the powerful women who are courageously awakening and making a difference in this world. The special women in my life, my Mum, my Angel Karen, my Soul Sister's, and Tribe of Warrior Women who continue to rise together. May our lights illuminate the path for future generations to follow. I love you with all my heart.

ABOUT THE AUTHOR

CAROL-ANN REID

Carol-Ann Reid is a Life and Business Mindset Coach who helps heart-led individuals heal and release their inner limitations, get clarity on their life purpose, and create a strategy for success. Known as 'first aid for the soul', she uniquely activates others' personal power and potential, awakening their authenticity and inner Warrior.

During her previous career as a professional singer and performer, Carol-Ann was drawn to help her peers manage their performance anxieties and found she had a natural talent for coaching. Six years ago, as a strong advocate for positive mental health and mindset, she retrained in Neuro-

Linguistic Programming, Cognitive Behavioural Therapy, Time-Line Therapy, Hypnotherapy, and Life Coaching. Carol-Ann now effortlessly combines her professional skills and intuitive abilities to be a true inspirer of change.

A lover of light and freedom, Carol-Ann lives her life as a Warrior Woman. Her heart-focused way of life means she boldly takes her twin toddler sons on never-ending adventures, indulges her wild side at the front row of rock concerts, and honours her spiritual self by leading Warrior Women's Circles and Moon Ceremonies.

Carol-Ann is available for powerful and transformative one-to-one coaching, group healing and activating programs, public speaking appearances and wellbeing workshops, and is the expert host of 'The Warrior Academy', her thriving online coaching membership.

You can connect with Carol-Ann at:

Email: hello@carolannreid.com

Website: www.carolannreid.com

Join the Awakened Warrior community on Facebook:

Awaken the Warrior Within

facebook.com/Carolannreid

instagram.com/carolannreidcoach

linkedin.com/in/carolannreid

2

EMBRACE YOUR INNER GODDESS

AMBER HARRISON

> " *Your vision will become clear when you can look into your own heart. Who looks outside, dreams. Who looks inside, awakes.* "

— CARL JUNG

I love the lightness and power that my spiritual awakening has given me. It's like a return, a deep sigh of "you've got this". It's an all-encompassing feeling that it's not just me anymore, struggling to cope, feeling alone, lost, disempowered, bewildered, overwhelmed and confused. There's a whole support system I can tap into that I'm a part of, that I've always been a part of. And the best bit? It's not an exclusive club! Every single one of us is in it, automatically, for free. It's up to each of us to decide whether or not to reconnect to it.

This connection I have is truly incredible. I simply close my eyes, place my hand gently on my heart and I can sense Spirit calling to me, reaching out, calming, healing, and grounding me.

I love my heart. I love my Self. Everyone I've ever loved is right there with me. My ancestors are there and all the future generations too. I know this might sound a bit cheesy but all the billions of people in the world are also in there. My heart is more than capable of holding space for each and every person as I am a part of The Universe, Spirit, Source; whatever you prefer to call it.

As I write this I'm in my early fifties and waking up every morning for me is a joy. I choose to set my alarm for 6.30 am. I choose to take a full hour, just for me, before I interact with the rest of the world; no checking my phone just yet. I choose a gentle ten-minute yoga routine to give my body a well-needed stretch. I choose affirmations that resonate deeply within me. I choose to connect to my Higher Self and call in the Archangels to protect, inspire, and guide me throughout my day. I choose to pull an oracle card and journal on the theme.

After this, my own, unique, daily spiritual practice, I'm connected, centred, grounded, and relaxed. I feel deep self-love and self-compassion. Having honoured my Self first, I'm ready to leave my bedroom to start my day.

My wish for you, gentle reader, is to find your *own* path to awakening, in a way that resonates with *your* soul. A path you can meander along that's full of reconnection to your Self, your inner wisdom, but also a deeper connection to something much bigger than just you. The Universal energy that we are all so much a part of.

Until my spiritual awakening, I only had fleeting moments where I felt truly connected. The bliss of a long candle-lit bath, a walk through a beautiful wood or along a blustery beach would nudge something from deep within me, but I was so disconnected to my Self I couldn't recognise it as my soul feeling nourished. My whole life was built around trying to work out why I didn't have those moments *all* the time. What was I doing wrong?

If you've been drawn to read this book then it is likely you are searching for a way back to your inner power. A positive, vibrant power that was there when you were small but you've lost through burnout, or it has been hacked away at by tough life experiences and lots of negative self-talk and thoughts. Maybe a constant, niggling fear holds you back or perhaps you've found yourself questioning whether your life is heading down the right path. Do you suffer from anxiety and low self-confidence that holds you back time and time again? Have you misjudged potential life partners and found yourself in awful, possibly abusive, relationships because you're "too trusting of others"? You love your children but motherhood is the hardest challenge you've ever faced, and it continues to be as they get older, but you're scared to admit it to yourself? Have you read loads of self-help books, watched endless programmes, studied courses, had therapy or counselling, talked to your friends and family but still don't feel any better? Maybe you've gone it alone and been the most perfect you can be in your job, with your family, your friends, and you've finally had enough of pretending. Perhaps you've lived for years knowing that there's something key missing from your life but no matter what you do, you just can't find it.

Eurgh...I've been there, and it was exhausting. I felt totally drained 99% of the time. I was being taught the same life lessons over and over, but there was a huge brick wall in front of me, stopping me from being able to release, accept, learn, and live.

In 2020 I turned 50 and my daughter tried to end her life. I couldn't cope any longer. I had what Brené Brown, international speaker on vulnerability, calls "a mid-life shake up". Why? Because I wasn't living my life's purpose. I faced a crossroads. I changed direction. I walked a different path.

I awakened spiritually.

It is my belief that every person is born awakened. As babies, we use all our senses to build up a story of what life is made up of. Our childhood experiences give us the baseline, unconscious and conscious stories we tell ourselves throughout our lives. These can be positive; I'm funny, I'm happy, I'm great at sports, or negative; I'm stupid, I'm an idiot, I can't do maths. You get the idea.

The positive stories serve us immense platefuls of inner joy. From this, we get contentment, fulfilment and it's easier to discover our purpose in life. But, what happens to us when we tell ourselves negative, disempowering stories? We fall asleep spiritually, as we only pay attention and listen to our mind. Mentally, we build up layers and layers of negative coping strategies that block out access to our inner voice, our intuition, our wisdom.

What's the number one priority for our mind? To keep us safe from harm. This stems back thousands of years in human evolution. All those years ago, we had to decide instantly how we were going to react to a potentially harmful situation. There was no time for thinking it through, we just had to act. The limbic system in our brain looks after all this without us having to do anything consciously. Whilst this can be life-saving by instantly getting the body's fuel pumps going with adrenalin, to either make us run away from danger or stay and fight, it's not so helpful when, for instance, it's triggered by someone loudly voicing their strong opinion, which takes you right back to when a parent unexpectedly raised their voice at you as a vulnerable child.

Now, as an adult, you know that, rationally, there's nothing to fear, but you might end up cowering and feeling worthless, unable to think as the adrenaline is flooding your system. Fear and anxiety reign supreme, stopping you from taking the action needed to dissolve the adrenaline. This is exactly what your mind wants, as now that you're unable to do anything, you're safe from harm. Your mind has won the

EMBRACE YOUR INNER GODDESS

battle once more. As we only have conscious access to 5% of our mind, the other 95%, tucked away in our subconscious, is always going to be louder and more oppressive. This much larger part continues running its familiar programs, stories and self-talk time and time again, but especially if there's even the faintest hint of change coming. This is where the first of my three Spiritual Awakening Tools comes in.

SPIRITUAL AWAKENING TOOL 1: SWITCH OFF YOUR BUSY MIND AND CONNECT TO YOUR BODY.

When you're stuck in negative thought cycles, telling yourself the same horrible stories round and round, it's crucial to begin your reconnection to your Self by first gently relaxing the body. You're aiming to switch off the body's automatic fight / flight / freeze / fawn response for a while. I'm going to teach you the technique I use. It's my top go-to, as I can do it whenever and wherever I want, and for as short or long as time allows. It's called 7/11 breathing.

The best way to learn and practice this powerfully gentle relaxation technique is by lying down, when you're in bed, ready to go to sleep, ideally with your eyes closed. Put one hand on your chest and one on your belly. Start breathing in through your nose whilst counting to 7, then breathe out through your mouth whilst counting to 11. Fill up your belly with your in-breath as though it were a balloon inflating. Now breathe out making the balloon deflate. Make sure you keep your chest still.

This might feel really odd. As adults, we generally take shallow breaths via our chests, but watch a baby and it's only their belly that rises and falls.

Keep breathing like this for at least 20 minutes, or until you fall asleep. The more you practise this the better. After practising this for 66 consecutive nights you'll be a pro at it. Now, when I do 7/11 breathing, my body knows exactly what's happening and in under a minute I'm connected, calm and relaxed. I use it when I'm driving, standing in a queue, before an important phone call, or walking in the door of somewhere new. My regular use is at specific points throughout my daily spiritual practice.

Why does this work?

The longer out-breath stimulates the parasympathetic nervous system to flood your entire body with relaxation. The counting is done to distract your mind. If you get lost counting simply start with the in-breath again and count to 7. Go at your pace of breathing and counting. Take time to find the rhythm that suits you.

OK, so that's how to help switch off your busy mind and relax your body. But what about reconnecting to your spirit?

Before I was 11 years old my spirit showed itself in creative ways, although being so young I didn't recognise it as that. I used to spend soul-enriching, creative time at my grandparents home. My parents were regularly commuting to a barn they'd bought to slowly convert and make into a habitable home, so my grandparents helped by having my sister and I stay. They had a wonderful garden with fields surrounding it. I remember hearing curlews calling from the long grasses. There was a meandering stream behind the flowers and vegetables. My grandpa rigged up a rope swing over it and I swooped over the water feeling the wind on my skin. I'd run about naked on the grass in the summer rain feeling incredibly alive and free. My granny made all sorts of soups and baked delicious cakes. She showed me how to do batik on white T-shirts. There was an incredible cupboard under the stairs with a wondrous dressing-up box. I could be anyone I liked and in my world I was Peter Pan a lot! I'm so very grateful for those early creating experiences and treasured memories of freedom, where anything seemed possible.

My childhood didn't feature any formal religion. There was no spiritual path shown to me by the adults surrounding me and, at times, I struggled to find my own way. It was the 1970s. I could roam around for hours wherever I liked, with no mobile, no one monitoring my movements. I remember being incredibly aware of my senses whenever I went on a walk or a bike ride. I think I must have felt very connected to nature. I know I was able to feel calmer when I was on my own outside, lying down in the long grass looking at the sky, or flying down a hill on my bike.

At the start of my secondary school years, we had a big change in my family life and we moved a long way away to a large city. I was young and couldn't work out why this felt so incredibly awful. Much more than the house move, the family change, and the new school, there was also an inner loss that I couldn't voice.

I hated school. I felt misunderstood. I was bullied. I didn't know how to express how I felt and was super scared of showing my emotions. I did my best to become average and fade into the background. In the 1980s, teenagers were pretty much left to their own devices so it was fairly easy to blend into whichever crowd you wanted to belong to. I had no idea and drifted from group to group, seeking validation but not finding what I truly needed, what my soul was looking for.

My mind got me to practise and practise looking externally to protect me from all that was hurting me. Going over and over the same negative stories. I was on red alert all the time. I had asthma but started smoking to "fit in" at school. I played truant. I dated boys so I could focus on loving them, not my Self. I couldn't cope with the nice boys who saw the good in me, I'd ditch them and fall for the bad ones that wanted to control me in some way. Unhealthy relationships that didn't leave me any breathing space to reconnect to, and love, my Self.

I began to lose touch with my inner Goddess wisdom. Slowly, I started to fall spiritually asleep.

Over the next few decades, I perfected the art of deflecting my inner needs and allowed my Self to only look externally. I people-pleased. I easily talked my Self into doing things I didn't want to do. I let others take advantage of me in extremely destructive ways. I trusted others too quickly. I doubted my decisions constantly and blindly adhered to others' well-intentioned, but wrong, advice.

Sometimes, though, my spirit did win out over my mind.

In my twenties, I studied for a degree in Anthropology and Psychology. I became super intrigued by how other cultures made sense of their world. My soul wanted to explore and experience Shamanism but my mind told me it seemed like something so utterly primordial that had no place in the modern world. That was that. Shut down, don't go there, it's too scary. Subdued, after my degree I went back into the world of administration, oh, how my mind loved the safe predictability! Over the next 15 years I became an expert at admin but my soul quietly withered in the barren landscape of paperwork.

In my thirties, a dear friend handed me books on essential oils and ways to celebrate the pagan festivals. This sparked my soul's interest in working with nature and its cycles, the moon and tarot cards. Whilst working part-time, yes, in admin, I excitedly completed Diplomas in Aromatherapy, Flower Remedies, Nutrition, Herbalism, Life Coaching and Stress Management, thinking "this is it, this is the *real* me!" I bought a tarot card deck, dipped into it, and then, gingerly, put it down again. With all this potential to change and break free, my mind was massively panicking. It played its top card 'my job is to protect you' again. Defeated, I went back to admin and stayed, safely, under the radar.

Then, my two beautiful children chose me to be their Mum.

I'm pretty sure you're probably thinking from what you've read so far that getting pregnant was a great experience for me. Surely, by now, I'm in touch with nature and my Self? Well, I still wasn't fully committed. Despite all the learning I'd done, I was being ruled by the iron rod of my mind. Spirit hardly ever got a look in. I really didn't like being pregnant. My mind couldn't make sense of what was happening to my body and struggled to keep me safe from the growing child. I had postnatal depression for the first year with both of them. Coupled with ending up being a single mum, twice, motherhood didn't come easily to me.

My forties saw me bringing up two children alone, completing a Postgraduate Diploma in Psychotherapy, working in the unbelievably busy world of primary school administration, navigating the benefits system as I was on a low income and never, ever wanting to meet a man again. Remember I said earlier I dated boys as a way of being loved? Well, I got so very lost in that patriarchal idea that my Prince Charming would make everything right, that I fell into destructive relationship patterns which constantly repeated themselves and I'd had enough. Ah-ha! Look what just happened right then, a spirit moment popped up!

Yet, still, I couldn't shake off that feeling of being alone and was giving, giving, giving to others without giving to my Self. I was convinced that I simply needed someone to help me, to do it all for me, or better yet, take the pain away. At least that's what my protecting, controlling mind told me.

Others said; "You're strong", "You're independent", "You've done this before", "You'll be fine", "You've got no choice so just get on with it", "You're doing a great job'" "You've got over hard times before, you can do it again", "You'll be OK". But I wasn't even remotely OK. I was utterly shattered, fragmented. I didn't have a clue who I was or when I last made a decision that was mine alone and not based mostly on advice from someone else. I'd lost an enormous amount of confidence. I'd been in dire, life-changing situations before, but this time was different. My awakening was the only path left available to me.

MY AWAKENING.

When my daughter took an overdose, I was punched in the face with the horrifying fact that she might die. I was at work when I had a phone call telling me to ring my daughter as she'd just texted the caller to ask if taking 64 paracetamol in one go is too much. I listened in disbelief not knowing what to say. A million crazy thoughts rushed through my mind; "64? IS it too much?", "I'm at work I can't deal with this now", "Where is she?", "Is she alone?", "Will she even answer the phone to me?", "Is she still alive?". The caller said, "64 is way too much. Ring your daughter first to check she's still awake and then ring for an ambulance. Do it NOW."

My daughter had been suffering in so many ways mentally for the last four years. Up to this point she'd been dismissed as not being in a bad enough state to have CAMHS support, was battling bulimia and all its devastating effects, she'd been to A&E numerous times due to cutting, abused alcohol and drugs, had no control over her emotions and our relationship had been tested to its extreme limits.

My hands were trembling but I managed to make the phone call. She answered, sounding drowsy. I told her I was ringing 999 and to pack a bag as she'd have to go to A&E. I walked out of work, got into my car and started the three-hour drive to get to her. I went numb, dissociating from what was happening. I've retreated deep within like this before when I was in terrible situations. It was the only way I knew to get through. Keep everything at arm's length until my thinking brain catches up.

I stayed like this for three weeks. Then I stepped back, dropped out, and broke down as I just couldn't cope. I found it impossible to sustain my numbness. Something was pushing me to really FEEL into what I needed to change in order to make sense of what was happening. I thought I'd hit rock bottom in the past but this was far, far below the bedrock. I was drowning in molten lava and needed to get out to save what was left.

Over the next couple of months, I wandered around aimlessly, trying my usual coping mechanisms: being with my loved ones, having psychotherapy, going on long walks, being alone, taking time off from work, plus trying a new method - taking sleeping tablets, even though I hate taking any medicines. The pills knocked me out so much that I only took them for two nights. None of it was working. I had nearly lost my daughter. I was terrified. I desperately needed something bigger in my life - how else could I ever process something as devastating as that?

And then, instead of quietly sending whispers that I could so easily ignore, my soul got bold. *Really, really* bold. This was unlike anything I'd ever experienced before. I felt compelled to connect with an ancient knowing, to reconnect to my calling. I couldn't voice it at the time but I needed to tap into my light, my wisdom, my intuition. It began with intense screaming, coming from deep within me. It wouldn't be silenced. A guttural wail, an ancestral voice, all the women who'd lived before me gathering collectively to make me listen. Finally, listen. But to whom? To my inner Self, the Goddess within.

I now know what I was experiencing was my spirit awakening. You might know it better by the common psychological term - a mental breakdown. Everything I knew fell away. I couldn't do anything but write in my journal when my life collapsed. Work was impossible. How would I drive myself there, let alone concentrate? It was an effort just to get up, to shower and wash my hair. I had no idea about what meals to cook. I could hardly string a decent sentence together. I felt like my life was all blurry. I became a hermit, preferring my own company for several months, whilst I began rebuilding my life and healing in a totally different way.

My first Spiritual Awakening Tool taught you how to settle your mind and relax your body. Well, here's what spirit demanded me to learn next in my awakening, with zero excuses accepted this time.

SPIRITUAL AWAKENING TOOL 2: SETTING BOUNDARIES SO YOU CAN TRUST YOUR INTUITION.

This tool involves creating the essential personal boundaries you need to begin your spiritual path. As an empath, I sense others' energy when I walk past them or as I enter a room. It's taken me many years to realise this means I need super-strong boundaries to protect myself from energy drain. Until my breakdown, my boundaries were extremely fluid. I people-pleased, compared myself to others and played the "why me / poor me" card over and over. Self-doubt crept all over me and my confidence kept on plummeting.

Looking back, it's clear to me that spirit stepped in at this point and guided me to a magnificent book, Better Boundaries, by Jan Black. It's not labelled as a spiritual book but it gave me the boost of self-love that I so desperately needed and had been missing for me since my childhood. As I read, a realisation broke over me like a new dawn...

I couldn't help my daughter until I helped my Self.

After decades of ignoring my Self, I'd lost myself so entirely that I could no longer support my Self. Tenderly, I asked my intuition a question "what was it that I truly needed?" I waited quietly, patiently, and began to hear Divine whisperings from my soul giving me guidance to follow. My new, true, path was slowly unravelling before me.

I started by giving myself permission to trust my Self by creating personal boundaries that honoured my authentic Self. For the first time in my life, I gave myself fully over to my inner wisdom. "Trust in your Self" was my daily mantra and slowly, I did as I was telling myself. It was beautiful listening to and being guided by my intuition instead of being a slave, shackled to my fearful thoughts. I felt protected by spirit and was able to set boundaries that felt aligned with me. I practised saying 'no' and 'maybe' instead of always 'yes' by silently first checking in with my soul.

 In order for boundaries to be set, you first have to believe and trust in your intuition."

— AMBER HARRISON

As I gained my confidence in trusting my inner wisdom I was told to give my body a gift. I was drawn to an enlightened soul sister who gently massaged my back and gave me my first-ever session of Reiki. She told me all seven of my chakras were desperately unbalanced and gently helped to begin the healing process. I stood up so tentatively afterwards feeling like my head was full of concrete and my feet were lighter than air! The energy in my body had completely flipped around. I immediately booked another session with her but, this time, I went for an angel and tarot card reading plus Reiki. I'd dabbled in tarot and oracle cards a few years before and had my own decks, but yes, you guessed it, I'd stopped. The readings were detailed and gently guiding, and gave me so much to think about. More than that, though, my interest in card decks was rekindled.

Cue my last Spiritual Awakening Tool.

SPIRITUAL AWAKENING TOOL 3: RECONNECTING TO UNIVERSAL INTELLIGENCE.

Daily oracle card pulling and journaling have totally transformed my life. These practices provide me with an ever-deepening relationship with my Self and the universal intelligence that surrounds each and every one of us. Journaling is great for your mental health and spiritual connection as it engages the left, rational, analytical side of the brain, allowing the creative right side to play, dream and wander about. Oracle cards are a divination tool that has been used since ancient times. Their purpose is to help you have a dialogue with Spirit, Goddess, your Higher Self, whatever you prefer to call the vast universal intelligence, and so make sense of your past experiences, whilst offering guidance for the present and future.

Here's how I recommend you begin. Choose an oracle deck where you are drawn to the imagery. There are plenty of lovely ones to choose from on the internet. The deck will have a small guidebook giving the theme of each card. Start by shuffling the deck in whatever way feels comfortable to you. Think of a question or set an intention in your mind. When you sense it's right, stop shuffling and turn over the top card. Before you open the guidebook, have a deep look at the card. Try to connect with the imagery. Look at the colours and the shapes. Are there any figures or animals? What might the scents be like? Now read the card's theme. Pick up your journal and begin writing everything that comes up for you. Explore your feelings and thoughts. Write for at least five minutes daily. Over time, you will start to see patterns and spot guidance from Spirit.

 This above all: to thine own Self be true.

— WILLIAM SHAKESPEARE

This self-empowering quote found me when I was in a dark place. With all my heart, I encourage you to Follow Your True Path. Your life is yours alone to live. Don't compare your Self to anyone else as we're all at different stages. You offer the gift of being uniquely you. You deserve to show the world your inner light in whatever way deeply resonates with you. Spirit will help you, and I can support you in doing this. All you need is an open mind, a willingness to change, and the determination to go for it.

Finally, I would encourage you to start building your own spiritual toolkit. Use your curiosity to try out tools that work best for you in reconnecting to your inner Self. As well as the top three I've written about, some of my absolute favourites are working with the energies of crystals, the evocative scents of essential oils, the healing properties of the moon's cycles, being outside in nature every day, and listening to guided meditations. There are many other ways mentioned throughout the other chapters in this book. Work out what creates that spiritual connection just for you. Remember, there's no right or wrong when it comes to building your personal awakening toolkit. Take it slowly. You have the rest of your life to learn how to love your Self and build your very own connection to Spirit.

Gentle reader, I wish this for you as you awaken:

May your self-awareness blossom, your self-expression develop, your self-confidence soar, your self-belief rise up, and your soul feel tenderly nourished.

MY FIVE KEY TAKEAWAYS

1. *Be in flow.* Every day, do something that you get lost in, where time doesn't exist, that makes your soul soar. This raises your vibration, energy, and alignment. When you feel good, good things happen.

2. *Practice kindfulness.* A beautiful combination of being mindfully present and deep self-compassion, kindfulness significantly lowers stress and promotes pure relaxation. This gifts your body a well-deserved break from all the stress it's put under by your mind.

3. *Show gratitude.* At the end of your day think of three things you're grateful for, anything at all. As you drift off with positive thoughts, you've raised your energy and realigned yourself with Spirit.

4. *Use affirmations.* A well-chosen affirmation will resonate deeply within, often producing lightbulb moments, the impetus to change, and connection to your Higher Self.

5. *Learn how to deep breathe.* Give your mind, body, and soul time-out by learning and, importantly, using a technique like 7/11 breathing.

Dedication

I dedicate this chapter to my daughter, Millicent Rose.
My treasure, your darkest moment showed us the way to awaken to the light within; to embrace our inner Goddess.

ABOUT THE AUTHOR

AMBER HARRISON

Amber Harrison is a Self-Love Coach, Psychologist and Spiritual Path-Builder. She blends science and intuition to coach women who are searching to reconnect to their power-ful, spiritual self and start that new life chapter they are desperately longing for.

Before starting her coaching practice, Follow Your True Path, Amber survived destructive relationships, soul-destroying jobs and single-handedly brought up her two children. After experiencing burnout by struggling for decades to fit into a box that wasn't her true size, Amber now passionately coaches and empowers women to follow their true path in life, and embrace their authentic, feminine self.

Amber feels rejuvenated being in 'circle' with like-minded women, loves having adventures in Olive, her 1970 VW camper van, and indulges her inner child by driving a steam locomotive once a year. Sounding the whistle is one of her top five most favourite things in the world!

Amber is available for deeply-empowering Self-Love Coaching and advises on Spiritual Path-Building for beginners. Amber has a lust for learning. Keep a watchful eye on her in the future, as she expands her skillset to offer more and more to her community of authentic and finally-free women. Better yet, why not come and join in?

You can reach Amber at

Email: hello@followyourtruepath.com

 facebook.com/followyourtruepath

3

IS YOUR LIFE BEING STEERED BY A SIX YEAR OLD?

CARLY BOYLE

Piercing cries vacated the little girl's lungs, their magnetic force soaring towards my unsettled heartbeat. Clutching tightly to the discomfort that had inhabited my weakened body, her steady, infant whimpers fired electric shocks through my anxious veins. My digestive system seized up and countless trips to A&E saw me beg for a medical explanation. I felt suffocated by the pressure of my diaphragm. My legs felt like paper, folding beneath me. Here, in my adult existence, was the presence of a little child. She was contorted in pain as she called out to me from the depths of despair. A fractured, innocent soul, who was pinning for my tender love and unfaltering acceptance.

Completely unaware of what I was doing on a spiritual level, I had continually let this little girl down by denying her the gentle reassurance that she so desperately craved. Instead of walking alongside her, helping her to grow in knowledge, I selfishly belittled her. "For goodness' sake Carly, would you just concentrate! Read more and try harder, maybe then you will be smarter and not have massive gaps in your knowledge! You are embarrassing me. You're a teacher and you don't know the dates of the second world war or the name of the tree that those leaves have fallen from!" I scolded. My voice was dripping with disgust as my angry thoughts seeped like deep-rooted weeds into her innocent hazel eyes that were ten times too big for her little face.

Sometimes, her tiny fists clenched tightly together and, out of nowhere, she would beg me to run for safety. She felt like the world was closing in on her, fearing the crushing weight that accompanied the darkness. During these times, her spindly legs, mapped with bruises from endless cartwheeling, dug their heels sharply into my gut. Frantically stepping into her trainers, which lit up proudly across the heels, she star-jumped into my solar plexus, dragging my wine-flushed cheeks outside onto the terrace. Sitting in painful silence, we clung to the final rays of the sun, as it made its hasty descent behind the charcoal mountains. She was timid and afraid, but I heard courage roar from the bones of her tiny, fragile frame.

The little child doesn't belong to me, she is me. She is the rhythmic, gymnastics-obsessed, six-year-old me, who sports a dodgy bowl-like fringe and owns a classic Snatch the Dog duvet set. She collects trolls, and after styling their brightly coloured hair into perfectly formed cones, arranges them proudly on the pine shelf above her single bed. Clambering over the bars of a swing in the back garden, she throws the fluorescent orange seat overhead and hangs upside down from the frame allowing the blood to rush to her head.

On the outside, she is a successful gymnast, performing well in school and building meaningful friendships. Lurking below the surface, however, are deep, open wounds, carved into her soul, that travel with her every morning to school and onto the gymnastic carpet every time she competes. Painfully shy and uncertain, she exists in fight or flight mode, but she wears it so gracefully that you might never catch a glimpse of her profound unrest.

Finally, in my thirties, I have set six-year-old Carly free. She is no longer crushed by the turmoil of her formative years and making adult life decisions for me. The turbulent emotions, stemming from an anxious attachment style have settled and I can proudly declare that she is safe, secure, and overflowing with childlike creativity. I would love for you to meet her, but in order to fully appreciate her zestful spirit, you must first place her tiny cold hand in yours, as she guides you through her awakening journey.

CARLY FARLY – LITTLE ME – ESTABLISHED 1987

I do not wish to cause pain to either of my parents by sharing my truth. No reader should feel shame for past decisions or situations they have found themselves in. Clothed with sensitivity and understanding, I will open this part of my story by declaring the most important lesson of my entire journey so far:

"It is never too late to rewrite the beginning."

My parents are an encouraging and loving influence in my life now, however, the suffering of my formative years had a snowball of effects on my life.

Making the journey Earthside, a baby's first gasp is quickly succeeded by a deafening wail as they cry out for safety, love, warmth and connection. As a child begins to grow and develop in a nurturing environment, their self-esteem blossoms. They are securely attached to their loving, available parents and they go on to have healthy adult relationships, living happily ever after…

except…

wait a moment,

let's rewind and reflect.

The reality for most is rarely close to the idyll that nature intends. Every one of us has been born into a certain time, to particular parents, in a unique set of circumstances - variables, outside of our control.

My mother and father have both fought with their own demons in this lifetime, none of which are mine to disclose. The circumstances that I was born into resulted in my first months on earth being spent in foster care - a time that I hold no memory of, but trusting in science, the neural pathways of my brain do. Without placing a heavy emphasis on the darkness of my childhood, for it no longer holds power over me, a brief overview will give context to my healing journey. When I was six years old, a partner moved into my mother's home; his aggressive and volatile outbursts sent shudders of fear rippling through me.

This man, who spent over a year living with us, sexually abused me. He also forced me to witness violent acts as he held a knife to my mother's throat in the kitchen of our home. Frantically running from one side of the house to the other, I finally managed to unlock the front door of our terraced house before he caught me, racing barefoot through the streets for help. Throughout this time, and the subsequent years, I became frightened of everything - even something as insignificant as misplacing my school jumper - for fear of getting in trouble. I didn't have a relationship with my father during these years of my life and my mother's mental health spiralled after the death of my grandmother.

Burying what had happened to me, I continued with life, only disclosing the abuse when I was 11 years old. This man had long gone from our lives and I was 'past it'. After attending children's counselling, I grew up convinced the abuse hadn't affected me and found myself delighting in my "strength" - no flashbacks or long nights spent trembling over my unfortunate encounters, so I was fine, right?

Truthfully, I was miles from being at peace, but I had yet to make the connection with the emotionally unavailable partners I would go on to choose, or my gut-wrenching determination to make unhealthy relationships last. Familiarising myself with the pattern that had deeply ingrained itself into my subconscious took years:

"You aren't loveable Carly, you aren't enough for him, he will get bored. Check your phone because he will text and break up with you. Oh look, he has texted, it's ok, he still loves you for now." I failed to hear myself speak these thoughts at the time - only hindsight provided me with a clear understanding. My bodily sensations confirmed that my inner child was hearing these damaging lies screaming from within. The key driving force behind the relationships I choose was my negative self-belief and lack of self-love for the little girl who looked to me for safety.

The only way out of this harrowing existence was to delve inward, but how?

DID YOU KNOW THERE ARE ONLY SEVEN STORIES IN THE ENTIRE WORLD?

My experience of spirituality involves connecting to something beyond my physical existence, to bring about internal change. It required learning how to bypass my cognitive thinking brain to access the heart seat of my spirit, the dwelling of my inner child. My spiritual awakening that allowed me to bring my inner child home wasn't linear, but a journey that meandered throughout the entire decade of my twenties and remains ongoing.

Reading a scientific book, listening to an informative podcast, or being present in the moment enriches my understanding of spirituality, while in the past, meditating on the word of God slowly began to shake my negative belief system. Icy cold water cascaded over my face and salty tears gently kissed my lips as I was baptised on Northern Irish shores. It was a crisp October day when my lungs cried out that I believed. I had just turned 26 when I accepted that God would find a purpose for my pain. I trusted in His plan to give me life in abundance.

 You intended to harm me, but God intended it for good to accomplish what is now being done."

— (GENESIS 50 V20)

This particular verse vibrated through my mind and heart, fuelling me with steadfast hope that I previously never had. Giving power to those words, along with other passages from the bible enabled me to confidently return to education, attain the grades required to study at university, and five years later, graduate as a teacher. Being faced with tutors telling me it was impossible to get to where I needed on my particular course forced me to turn inward, declaring that with God, anything was possible. Today I believe that:

 Whatever you give power to, has power over you."

I was completely oblivious that my inner child was listening, for I had yet to discover her existence. Regardless, just as a tiny human with a ketchup-stained chin lingers at their parent's heels, Little Carly clung to every word and thought expressed. Possibly perplexed to hear me speak positive words over myself, she remained anxious and fearful of the inconsistency I provided. Change takes time and growth requires patience.

Your personal awakening journey may or may not kick start under the promise from a god, but however your story begins is completely beautiful and perfect for you. It is about accepting that there is more to life than the physical world we can see and touch in front of our eyes. During my first year at university, a lecturer explained that there are only seven basic narrative plots in all storytelling. Their frame-works, which are recycled repeatedly, may be decorated by different settings, characters, and conflicts, but the plot remains unchanged. There is no wrong way to script your spiritual journey and meet with your inner child, however, one core element of the story will remain universal:

 You cannot think your way out, you must BE the way out for your inner child."

The years rolled by and my self-awareness blossomed. Reading books on attachment theory strengthened my understanding of my behavioural patterns. Drinking endless cups of coffee with women from prayer groups inspired and encouraged me. However, frustration lingered. Despite being armed with information that gave me insight into who I was, Little Carly remained jumping up and down, begging me to choose her. Instead, I chose a 1500-mile move across Europe to the Island of Mallorca. Love would set me free.

FAST FORWARD TO 2019 - THE BEGINNING OF THE END

Pacing back and forth over the freshly vacuumed ceramic tiles, the Spanish sunshine poured into our family apartment. Everything felt a little lighter when the smell of furniture polish lingered gently in the air and the mountain of clean clothes that had stiffened in the scorching heat had been folded and neatly tidied away. I was 32 years young. My wedding album resembled a bridal magazine and I had given birth to a perfect, 6lb 2oz, wrinkly-nosed baby boy the year prior. Life on my Instagram grid was picture-perfect.

Intoxicated with the notion of marriage, I had believed that a family unit would bring me a sense of wholeness and belonging, yet, here I stood, alone on a small balcony at the front of our home, and as dusk painted the sky shades of pink and purple, I felt as empty as the rows of derelict hotels that lined the ghostly quiet Mallorquin streets in the height of the pandemic. The chirping of crickets echoed loudly as I finally swallowed the truth, admitting to myself that I had promised my life to someone whose values didn't align with my own. I had contorted myself to fit into his world, unaware that my wounded inner child had taken the reigns of my adult decisions.

Her turbulent emotions, a product of her unmet needs in childhood, were much stronger than any wisdom I had accumulated through life experience. The discomfort from my crippling IBS was an outward symptom of her inner turmoil. My desire to keep everything clean and in order, including my eating habits, were another external display of the fraudulent foundations that formed the architecture of my life. Reality weighed heavier than ever, yet somehow, it stirred light and hope in my heart.

Coming to the end of myself felt different. Comfortably exhausted from the anxiety that chased at my heels to every destination, I felt an eagerness to dispose of the neediness that radiated from my essence. The energy to cling to emotionally unavailable partners, wondering if I was good enough, pretty enough, or funny enough to keep their attention had evaporated. I had placed boyfriends on a pedestal, yet as the dust settled, the absence of common ground was uncovered. As a deep thinker who enjoys the simplicity of life and values wisdom, I hadn't considered holding out for a partner who would mirror this. Truthfully, I didn't choose my partners, I was drawn to them and infatuated by them, a reflection of what I had experienced growing up.

It was at this moment, that a flame ignited within my soul and my knowledge felt like it was flowing down into my heart, allowing me to surrender. My world was going to change dramatically and although the road ahead was set to be extremely messy, tears of relief filled my eyes and I felt a sudden burst of gratitude for my failed marriage. Acquiring everything I thought I needed to be happy had failed miserably, and it had brought me to the most beautiful place I had ever stood in. A place of readiness - ready to return home to Northern Ireland, a country that I couldn't wait to leave; ready to be alone, a set-up I had dreaded for as long as I could remember; ready to heal. It was like searching everywhere for your sunglasses, only to discover they are on top of your head all along. Relentlessly running to everything and everyone for my door to happiness and freedom, when all along the keys were right there in my hands. I had been spiritually aware for a very long time, but now, I was beginning to spiritually awaken. It was time.

My inner child heard my decision to leave. Reflecting on this moment, I feel like Little Carly climbed onto the purple frame of her bicycle and perched herself at the edge of the padded white seat. Holding tightly to the handlebars, which had pink and white ribbons streaming from the side of their rubber grips, she began trusting me to parent her. Wobbling initially with uncertainty, we pressed on through the paved streets and she slowly loosened her grip, passing control back to me. With every turn of the pedals, my heart unknowingly wrapped around hers and the chasm between the levels of consciousness that we were existing on began to close.

BACK TO NORTHERN IRELAND

Held in Spain by marital promises and giving birth under Spanish law, I stepped onto the scary path of uncertainty that lay ahead of my decision to leave. An explosion of a court case followed back in Northern Ireland. Three repatriation flights later, my life, and Noah's, were squeezed into a suitcase and, I'll be honest, without legal permission to rebuild over here, I fled. No job, no house, and petrified of being ushered on a plane back to Spain.

The only time my nervous system was ever in a slightly regulated state was when I was out in nature, exploring with my then-two-year-old son. Stripped of material possessions, rarely caring for make-up because what did it matter when you were being taken to court for a custody battle, I spent the majority of my time outdoors. Hair tied back, any clean clothes thrown on me that I could find sprawled across my mother's bedroom, Noah and I were outside, regardless of weather conditions.

Embarking on the scariest rollercoaster I had ever been on before, my inner child healing had already begun. Please find comfort in knowing that if you are currently shoulder deep in the muckiness of life; the kind of mud your feet sink speedily into, you can decide to roll in it like a two-year-old would. I promise that your spiritual self could be prospering, for we don't always awaken in the light but require a time of darkness so we can learn exactly where to find the light.

THE REPARENTING MANUAL

These are the steps I have taken to bring peace and harmony to Little Carly. The difference in my journey is that I didn't carry out all of these tasks in hope of acquiring inner child healing; it was actually a reverse process. It was a natural path that I found myself stepping onto, with only hindsight allowing me to see the impactful effects of these actions. Consequently, I can promise with utmost sincerity that they can provide a channel for you to get in touch with your inner child, allowing you to meet with that innocent soul and begin to reparent them. Consider these ideas with an open mind and reject the urge to cognitively comprehend them. These activities aren't designed to flatter the conscious mind but instead are there to reprogramme the subconscious - the part of our mind that is incapable of reasoning and is therefore non-judgmental and flexible. This brings me to step one:

- **Buy the welly boots** - It was a blustery November morning in Northern Ireland. The sort of day that makes the rims of your ears ache from the cold and there is immense difficulty seeing two feet in front because of the rain pelting diagonally into your face. Noah was in nursery when my friend and I decided to take a walk up Cave hill in Belfast. Not owning a pair of walking boots, I trudged into M&S where I was sure to pick something up in a hurry. The brightest pair of boots in the shop was decorated with multi-coloured pastel hearts and hung splendidly in the children's shoe section. Those boots were the only boots for me. Bent over laughing in the queue to pay, my friend told me her five-year-old niece owned the exact same pair. I cannot emphasise the delight I had in buying and owning those boots enough. My feet were perched proudly on the dashboard for the entirety of the journey and we continuously erupted into fits of laughter at the ridiculousness of my boots. Over the coming months, I waded into the puddles wearing those boots, and my anxieties were cleansed in the muddy water. It was as if my adult concerns fell to the bottom of the water and the puddles transported me to a place of serenity. Those boots were the bridge I travelled over to arrive in the perfect land of imperfection. Little Carly hadn't experienced jumping in puddles before, but as the filthy water splattered over her rosy cheeks, Noah showed her that messy hair, dirty clothes and sparkling eyes were faultless.

- **Sensory experiences**- young children learn best when they are provided with multisensory experiences; my inner child was no exception to the rule. Blessed to have Noah as a role model, Little Carly found healing as she constructed race tracks from sand and marvelled at her extravagant creations. She screeched with enthusiasm as she counted how many times her smooth grey pebble skimmed across the shimmering water and delighted in fabricating make-believe food from play dough. Standing proudly at her kitchen window, she watched in amazement as the birds flocked to her back garden to enjoy the cluster of seeds that were smothered across the peanut butter on her homemade bird feeder. Carefully observe children at play, whether it be your own children or the little ones belonging to your friends and family. Allow their presence to encourage your inner child to surface. You will be amazed at the peace that can breed in an uncomplicated sensory activity. Fleeting thoughts will settle as your senses engage and your childlike enthusiasm emanates.

- **Find your cosy cosy -** After a long day of playing, my little boy takes his comfortable position on the sofa and pulls the fleecy mauve blanket tightly under his chin. Burying himself in my armpit, Noah declares that it is time to get 'cosy cosy.' I began to relish in this moment, knowing that as moonlight began to bathe the clouds, it was time to bask in precious tranquillity that warmed my heart and soul. Noah directed my inner child towards the satisfaction of unwinding in a place of safety. From this foundation, I began to hold my own space for relaxation by lining my fluffy pyjamas alongside his on the radiator. Little Carly began to trust my emergent love as I ran her warm baths topped with wispy bubbles after a long day and permeated the air in her room with delicate lavender mist from the diffuser that I bought for her. Placing a hot water bottle under her duvet and soothing her to sleep with a gentle meditation, my inner child became the centre of my existence. Fall in love with your inner child and begin to recognise her needs. You may hear her words expressed in the form of your bodily sensations and you may discern her emotional state in your snappy responses. Prioritise her needs above everything else and you will begin to familiarise yourself with her voice, even when she whispers softly. Call it a mother's intuition.

- **Inner child integration**- This was a planned session with the beautiful Carol- Ann Reid. I had been receiving coaching and was aware that the following week's session was set to be an inner child integration piece. I had attempted a similar hypnosis-style healing some years prior, but fear had unfortunately hindered its success. Previously frightened to let go and press into the meditative style state because anxiety and fear were my default, but this time around, I had found a coach I fully trusted. A state of readiness is perhaps the most significant factor and I was now beyond ready, I was ecstatic. During this session, my mind settled as I woke up in my childhood bed. Returning to that same terraced house, my adult self brought my inner child home. I held her, rocked her and skipped with her, hand in hand, as I integrated with my inner child and also my creative child. I cannot provide you with all of the details because the words and thoughts expressed seem to dissolve inward, but I can confidently tell you that this brought about another turning point in my journey. My inner child was already on her path to peace, now she was embodying confidence. Searching my kitchen cupboards to find Noah's confetti cannon, my instinct was to grab it and run outside. As the sky exploded with fireworks of rainbow paper, excitement rose from my diaphragm, the same place that once harboured fear and anxiety. I was excited about the future and no longer turned my head to look back. I only wanted to focus on what opportunities lay ahead.

A DAY IN THE LIFE OF NOW

Noah and I are settled in Northern Ireland. His father and I working hard to prioritise his needs. Marriage wasn't the solution, but forgiveness has been found in our parting of ways, as has an understanding of my faults throughout the separation process.

My inner child and I exist harmoniously, permitting life to unfold at its will. Afternoons roll cosily by and with graceful determination, I confidently knock on the doors that are aligned with my heart's desires. Accompanying the little girl whom I previously scorned to the library, she received her glossy purple membership card with great enthusiasm. My inner child rests contently beside Noah on the plastic green chairs in the children's section, feeling no shame for borrowing books on primary school history or garden birds to spot. Instead of demonising Little Carly, I provide her with rich learning experiences and following our adventures to museums or exhibitions, I rustle in my purse so that I can buy both Noah and I a souvenir at the end of the trip.

Going out for walks, I am no longer trapped inside a cycle of thoughts but instead, notice the water fizzing on the path as the smell of rain-drenched leaves float across my nose. The noises of my surroundings no longer startle me but the gurgling of the pipes, and the churning of the radiators that once made me question if an intruder was nearby, now add to my comfort of familiarity. Previously grimacing when someone paid me a compliment, a huge smile now spreads across my face, followed by a heartfelt thank you. Dread and worry have been replaced with childlike curiosity as I wonder what opportunities life will provide.

Challenging moments still arise and last night, I received an email notifying me that I hadn't been shortlisted for a job that I really thought I wanted. In the past, days of disappointment would have loomed over me as I questioned my ability, yet here I stand, inhaling deeply in the understanding that at this time, the role wasn't right for me. I am so content in my singleness that I almost forgot to mention it. Listening to my body and my inner child, I check in with myself regularly. Abolishing the idea of perfectionism, some days I exercise and experiment with plant-based cooking, while other days I cuddle up on the sofa with a takeaway.

I am my highest self. My most authentic self that now exists beyond my old, outdated coping mechanisms. I am connected to my intuition; going to me first for advice. My transformation has been so remarkable that I need to reintroduce myself, my name is Carly. I am a primary school teacher, proud single parent and aspiring Children's writer. One day, I watched Noah delight in smearing butter over the kitchen counters. Combining my passion for inner child healing with my love for children's literature, I transformed the mess of my kitchen into a Shakespearean sonnet. You can listen to my album on Spotify, which is an audiobook filled with poetry for children, based around finding joy in the ordinary. The stories range from watching cars outside the window to catching snowflakes in the garden.

Follow our journey and everyday life on Instagram @carly_- great_big_stories and watch this space for my first Children's book, which is currently in the making.

MY FIVE KEY TAKEAWAYS

1. Learn to recognise who is in the driving seat. Which version of you is steering your decisions?
2. It is never too late to rewrite the beginning.
3. You cannot think your way out of traumatic experiences, you must BE the way out for your wounded inner child.
4. Your spiritual awakening journey is a unique blend of the knowledge you acquire and the experiences you encounter.
5. The methods you use to connect to your spiritual side will likely evolve throughout your lifetime. Keep an open mind and a teachable heart.

Dedication

I would like to dedicate this chapter to my son Noah-Jax. Loving you unconditionally has taught me how to love myself. Thank you for showing me that healing can begin with the splash from a puddle and that happiness can be heard in the squelching of mud. Your energetic and curious spirit encourages me, your innate emotional intelligence takes my breath away, and your constant need to be on the go drives me to wine. You are a beautiful soul and I love you to the moon and back xxx

ABOUT THE AUTHOR

CARLY BOYLE

Carly is a primary school teacher, proud single parent and children's author.

She is passionate about fostering a child's love for stories and uses her creativity to enrich their reading journey. Observing her son Noah's favourite activities as inspiration, Carly created a poetry collection that was later recorded as an audiobook. She has also had her stories published in online magazines.

Before Carly embarked on her teaching career, she worked abroad as a dancer and entertainer. She is also a retired member of the British Gymnastics team and represented both Northern Ireland and Great Britain.

Carly adores listening to what experiences have shaped people's lives. She understands that our formative years are crucial to how we develop and ultimately, form our ability to have healthy, meaningful relationships with ourselves and others.

When Carly isn't enduring noisy play centres, she enjoys cooking chicken nuggets and spaghetti hoops on repeat, with an extra dollop of tomato ketchup. On other days, she cooks plant-based meals, spends time exploring in nature with Noah, and even manages to exercise. Carly has finally realised that perfection doesn't exist and inner child healing has enabled her to let go of her unrealistic expectations.

Combining her fierce love of inner child work and literacy, Carly has created children's stories that will engage and inspire the whole the family. These stories are on their way to being published.

You can find Carly on:

Spotify - great big stories for tiny wee people

instagram.com/great_big_stories
tiktok.com/@great_big_stories

4

LIVING A HEART-LED LIFE

WHEN NOT IGNORING YOUR INNER GUIDANCE UNCOVERS YOUR TRUE PATH

CAT MARSHALL

I thought I had it made! I was in my early 30s, had a lovely partner, a wonderful home, a rental house, a great job, a nice car. I spent Saturdays out with friends and Sundays wandering around garden centres, picking out a plant pot or two. Friends of mine used to comment on how well I'd done and how 'together' I was.

And to a certain extent, they were right… I studied hard and got a good degree from a great university; I put myself forward for challenging jobs which suited my hard-working and perfectionist nature; I took on more responsibility, got promoted and got paid excellent money; I had Andy, my kind, funny and handsome partner, as well as a beautiful home which we had bought and renovated together. All good right?

So why did I feel like something was missing?

I found myself with a pen in hand and a beautiful, crisp new notebook in front of me. I titled the page 'Things that would make happy changes in Cat's life'. First on the list: 'Buy clear stackable shoe boxes for my 27 pairs of high heels'. A few more minutes of deep introspection later, I skipped downstairs to make myself a cup of tea.

Waiting for the kettle to boil, I could feel something else bubbling inside me. "Shoe boxes are good," I thought, "but there's something bigger". Watching the tea swirl around the cup as I stirred, it came to me. "I could have my own business. That's the missing piece!"

And just like a fairy tale, it came to pass that one of my dearest friends invited me to set up a business with him. "How great is this? Could it be any better?" I thought to myself. "This time next year we'll be millionaires!"

I got straight down to doing what I do best: planning for every single eventuality that could ever happen. I discussed plans with Andy and we agreed he would support me financially while we launched the business. I handed in my notice at my job. I created a beautiful home office space. I spent hours researching the best-in-class options for everything I thought we'd need.

And just a couple of months into my business start-up adventure, more incredible news! Andy whisked me off for a romantic weekend together. He'd even booked a fancy, two-seater sports car for the occasion. "I'm so lucky!" I thought, "it's all coming together." We stayed in a beautiful, old hotel, we went on long walks followed by cosy drinks next to the fire in the local pub, and then, out in the open air surrounded by incredible views, he asked me to marry him.

I blurted out a 'yes', but as we jumped back into the car and my body came to rest on the leather seat, instead of feeling excited I felt a sense of emptiness, the dull ache of 'is this it?' A feeling that something wasn't right but I couldn't put my finger on it. Ignoring this feeling, I shoved my reservations in a box in my head marked 'don't worry about it now' and got on with making phone calls to my nearest and dearest.

The months that followed were a blur. The initial excitement was replaced by the feeling of a rock in the pit of my stomach weighing me down. On paper, we had everything... but it wasn't enough! The thought of resigning myself to this mundane life felt like I was putting myself in a cage. Andy and I worked on it, but it became clear there would be no wedding. What had taken eight years to build was destroyed overnight. I walked away, losing everything that was stable in my life: my relationship, my home, my financial security, my social circle. All the big pillars holding me up, making me 'who I was', were gone. I've never felt so completely adrift in my whole life.

I found myself sitting alone in a rented house, on the cold, hardwood living room floor (I had no furniture), drowning my sorrows in copious amounts of chocolate and red wine. My laptop sat in front of me. I started typing … "What do women do when they are nearly 40, have lost everything, and realise they will never have kids of their own?"

I felt the tears coming. Hot, stinging, resentful tears. One of the things that hit me hardest was the intense grief I felt over never having my own children. The thoughts wouldn't stop; "what if that was my one chance and I missed it? What if I meet someone now and there's not enough time? What if I can't even get pregnant? I'm getting older every minute!"

Mindlessly clicking around the internet, trying to find uplifting articles to bring me some hope, I came across a retreat to Bali for female entrepreneurs. Holy bat-balls, Batman! This was just what I needed to get me back on track. The only spanner in the works was, I didn't have the money to go. Undeterred, and fuelled by more chocolate and red wine, I made a deal with myself. I'd apply for a 0% credit card, and if I got it, I'd go to Bali! My fingers hit the keyboard with details of my application and I held my breath as I clicked the 'submit' button... Congratulations! Your shiny new credit card is on its way.

What did I have to lose? I knew that something drastic needed to change and I decided this was it. I soon found myself on a flight heading to a side of the world I'd never been, to meet a group of women in business I didn't know. I was determined to squeeze every single ounce I could out of this adventure.

We were treated to the most divine and healing experience I could have imagined. We were immersed in yoga, Balinese healers, and Tibetan singing bowls. I found myself gifted the most beautiful silver prayer ring, with an inscription to Lakshmi, the Goddess of abundance and fertility. Group meditations under palm trees and business planning by the pool were our every day. I looked around at the other incredible women there and felt like an imposter. Who was I to be here? What did I have that was special? Did I really think I could be successful?

My business partner and I were working all the hours and despite wanting to create a 'lifestyle' business, we had created the most intense and stressful 'jobs', which ruled our lives. We had a business that made no money and only had a handful of clients. My heart sank. Whatever we did, we couldn't get our business off the ground. Returning from Bali, I threw myself into work, doggedly determined that things would change for the better.

Christmas rolled around and it was time to take stock. From the outside, it looked like I should have been having the time of my life, but instead I was overweight, depressed, stressed and lonely, consumed by my failing business but feeling powerless to change anything.

I reflected on my journey and realised I was spending time doing things I felt I 'should' do to get a particular result. I decided it was time to do stuff for me. Stuff I wanted to do. Things that pushed me out of my comfort zone and FELT good. In a previous life, I'd reached the rank of First Dan

Black Belt in karate, so it felt aligned to find a mixed martial arts club and get fit again.

On the first night at my new club, I made my way nervously onto the mats. Looking around I saw eighteen big, tall, muscly men; all in tight, mostly black t-shirts and shorts with words like 'killer' and 'extreme' on them. The head coach, Matt, explained to me that this session was all about choke holds. I must have looked petrified as he asked "would you like me to get Amy to partner with you?" and before I could even think about it, I heard "no, no it's fine!" coming out of my mouth. As we partnered up, a guy called Will offered to help me. He was kind, patient and took the time to explain what we were doing as his arm clenched tighter around my neck. His smell was intoxicating and there was a definite spark between us. I finally felt the excitement of life returning!

It wasn't long before training became a solid fixture in my life, closely followed by Will. He was 10 years younger than me but I wasn't looking for anything serious, we just had a great time together. One morning I woke up with zero energy, I couldn't even get out of bed to make a cup of tea. Maybe I was sick? Something was pulling at my thoughts and my brain started working overtime... "Could I be pregnant?" It was only that one time we were careless and I thought at my age that would be virtually impossible! I raced to the pharmacy for a pregnancy test. I didn't have to wait long for the result... 'pregnant'.

Oh sh*t.

This was a disaster. I'd lose the business! I had no money and no support. I had a rental house I couldn't afford. I hardly even knew this man! I felt destined for single motherhood and years of scraping by on government benefits. With thoughts of impending doom clouding my mind, something was nudging me to check the calendar. It was exactly 12 months to the day that I was given the silver prayer ring in Bali! The one with the inscription to Lakshmi, Goddess of abundance and fertility. This 'coincidence' sent a wave of comfort through me, as I felt through every cell of my body 'this is how it's meant to be'.

I let nature decide my course and a few months later Will and I welcomed our first son, Marshall, into the world. Circumstance forced me to give up my business and landed me firmly in the new and uncharted waters of motherhood.

During my pregnancy, Will decided that he needed to get a 'proper' job to support our family, working as an assistant in a school wasn't enough. He had always dreamed of becoming a firefighter, so he applied all over the UK but with no luck. With our new baby just a few weeks old, he received a phone call: "There's a place for you at firefighter training school, but you'll have to start in a few weeks' time. You'll be away for four months, then you'll get stationed where we tell you."

I could feel the fear creeping up inside me. He'd be halfway across the country! I was already struggling and now I'd be alone and unsupported with a newborn. We couldn't afford to keep the house, so where would we go? We had no other options; simply put, we had to make it work. Will packed his bags, leaving me with a newborn and a house full of stuff to put into storage.

I packed my life into my little car with the leaking sunroof and found myself living between parents' and friends' houses with a baby in tow. I was a new Mum, clueless, sleep-deprived, and isolated, with an extremely challenging baby, spending life on the road without a place to call home.

What started out being four months, ended up being nearly a year. Every month, I waited for news on the location of Will's new job so we could move somewhere together, and every month there was nothing. One hot and frustrating day, the angst and sheer desperation of our situation truly got to me. I pulled my car over to the side of the road, Marshall sleeping in his car seat, and I cried. Tears were pouring down my face. All I could think was "how on earth does anyone survive raising a baby?" I literally couldn't do it anymore.

I poured my heart out. I was crying, questioning, bargaining; then I got mad. I was done. Something had to change. Facing up to the sky I told the Universe "Are you listening to me Universe? This stops NOW. You've got 24 hours to give me one massive sign. I need you to do SOMETHING! And I need it NOW!!" Did I expect anything to happen? In all honestly, probably not. But less than 24 hours later Will got a call and I got the sign I'd asked for; we were told where he'd be stationed. Relief and gratitude flooded through me – I'd been heard!

I immediately jumped online and started looking for somewhere to rent. Finding a place near enough to the station so Will could be 'on call' at night was impossible. After searching and searching, I was becoming so stressed, Will told me "Just give it a rest for a week or two, something will turn up". I reluctantly agreed.

A couple of weeks later, I was fast asleep in the middle of the night and a voice which wasn't mine popped into my head and said 'you must look on the internet now'. I woke up, wondering what on earth that was about and grabbed for my phone. As soon as I searched properties to rent, there it was… our perfect little family home.

Within a short time, I'd arranged a viewing, travelled across the country and was standing in 'our' living room - small but perfectly formed. I remember realising we're often shown tangible evidence of the Universe guiding us in the form of repeating numbers, especially 1s, and this time the sign was as plain as day – our new address was 111 Tudor Gardens.

Our new life in what I called our 'Universe House' was unfolding, but I was truly feeling the overload of full-on motherhood and sleep-deprivation. Unpacking boxes, I came across a pack of angel cards that I'd bought years before. The pack was deep purple and the title promised 'Daily Guidance from Your Angels'.

I shuffled the cards asking them "what do I need right now?" As if by magic a card popped out of the deck. The message was 'Energy Work'. Over the coming days, the same card kept popping out whenever I shuffled. I started searching for an 'energy worker' and, as luck would have it, I found Ruth Jones, a healer who wasn't that far from me. Over the coming months, I had a session with her every chance I got. She did all sorts of things I had absolutely no understanding or experience of, like energetic clearing, chakra rebalancing, Reiki, and shamanic healing. It reminded me so much of what I'd experienced in Bali and I always felt incredible when I left!

Soon, our little family welcomed another baby boy, Kolby, into our world. We had a homebirth again and weren't due to see any midwives, but I wanted some breastfeeding help, so we ended up taking an unscheduled trip to the maternity ward in our local hospital to see if they could give me some guidance.

There, I met an incredible midwife who took us under her wing. She had concerns about Kolby's breathing, but these were dismissed by doctors and consultants who gave him a clean bill of health. She wasn't convinced however, and he was admitted to the High Dependency Unit where he was diagnosed with congenital pneumonia and suspected sepsis. Phew! It felt like we had our angels looking after us that day! After a couple of days, he was transferred to the Special Care Baby Unit to continue his recovery, and soon we were allowed home.

Then, just two weeks later, we noticed a huge and sudden growth on the top of Marshall's leg, so off he went with Will to the A&E department. Another hospital admission later, he was sent for an operation to remove the abscess the next day, and a few days later was discharged.

We were only a few weeks into life as a family of four and we'd already had two hospital admissions, but I could tell that Will was getting itchy feet again. Alongside his full-time job, he'd also been sponsored to compete in the Street Luge World Cup Series and had already travelled around the globe to compete in eight races that year.

I honestly couldn't face him being away again after all we'd been through, but with a shot at the world title, it was an opportunity too good to miss. So, with an eight-week-old babe in arms and a two-year-old pulling at my leg, we waved goodbye to Daddy as he set off for South America. My only mission was surviving the few weeks he was away and keeping the kids in one piece.

One night, Kolby would not stop screaming; he was so distressed and I couldn't do anything to calm him. Walking around, trying to rock him, cuddle him, feed him, talk to him, sing to him, was getting me nowhere. I was desperately trying to hold it all together while Will was away, but I had a sixth sense telling me something was very wrong. I dropped Marshall at a friend's house in the early hours of the morning and headed to A&E where Kolby was admitted, this time, with suspected meningitis – our third admission in two months!

I watched as Kolby lay on the bed and a nurse set up his IV antibiotics. "Back in a moment" she told me brightly as she left the room. I looked at his little face, and within seconds his body started turning bright red. He looked like he was starting to expand like a balloon. His face contorted and blanched white, he was struggling to breathe. It took me a moment to realise what was happening.

I ran, yanked open the door and shouted "Can I get some help in here please!" Within seconds, a team of people were rushing into the room moving beds, grabbing oxygen masks, resuscitation equipment and administering adrenaline. I stood back, watching it play out; there was nothing I could do. I wondered if this was it? Would this be the moment that I watched us lose him? It seemed that time was suspended in that one moment, but the strange thing was, I didn't feel alone – it was almost as if I was being held by an invisible force.

Suddenly, he was screaming and screaming. I snapped back to reality and made my way through the team of people to pick him up and hold him. Thankfully, after what seemed like an eternity, he calmed down - he'd had an anaphylactic reaction to the antibiotics.

The early hours of the morning came and I watched as Kolby slept in his hospital cot next to me. Scrolling through social media sites, I kept being drawn back to a woman called Natasha Bray, talking about an incredible new type of hypnotherapy she was doing. I felt the urge to reach out and contact her, but it was 6am and I'd be calling from hospital – she'd think I was crazy! I messaged her anyway.

To my surprise, a message pinged straight back into my inbox… Natasha was with her sleeping child too and could talk now – apparently, I'd caught her at the perfect time. She told me how she was helping people transform their lives and businesses using hypnotherapy. I felt a nervous excitement in my belly – this called to me so much! My mind was made up – I'd sign up to take an in-depth course on transformation and become a Certified Hypnotherapist. Perhaps something incredible would come out of this after all.

I felt genuine relief when I realised we'd got through what I considered to be our 'three things' with the boys. After all, things come in threes, don't they? Life finally looked like it was calming down and we'd just moved into a new home, coincidentally another 'Universe House'.

I was struggling to adjust to being a new mum of two small boys, but was guessing that was a pretty normal state to be in. Marshall was nearly three and his behaviour was exhausting! Frequent meltdowns, screaming, crying – I couldn't do anything with him. He started developing a range of seemingly unconnected symptoms; random vomiting, night sweats where he woke up screaming and soaking wet, and when I picked him up, he shouted "Mummy hurting me!" He was extremely lethargic, stopped wanting to walk anywhere and virtually stopped eating. Within weeks the bubbly two-year-old I knew was a shadow of his former self.

After taking him to the doctor several times, with the usual 'he's got a new sibling', 'he's got a virus' type suggestions, I knew in my gut something wasn't right. I asked what tests we could carry out because we needed answers and soon. By the time I was standing in hospital, waiting for blood tests, I knew I had to talk to a specialist paediatrician.

I was told by several staff members that I'd have to go back and get a referral from our doctor, which could take weeks, but thankfully, a nurse walking by overheard my conversation and decided to help – another healthcare angel sent to look after us! The consultant we saw immediately ordered a raft of blood tests and told me they'd rush them through. Six hours later, we received a phone call; "you need to come back to the hospital. Please come now".

36 hours and two hospital transfers later, with Marshall admitted to the specialist paediatric oncology unit, Will and I were ushered into a small, brightly coloured playroom as a play therapist carried Kolby in the other direction. Dr Connor, our consultant, followed us in and sat down; "Your son has Acute Lymphoblastic Leukaemia, a type of blood cancer". "What does that actually mean?" I heard my voice ask. He proceeded to explain with kindness and patience what it meant, where we were and what was going to happen next. He told us "Without treatment, we would estimate that

your son has 6-8 weeks to live". It was hard to even process the words he was telling us.

What we thought we knew, the life we were expecting to happen tomorrow and the next day and the day after that, was ripped from us in an instant. We were thrown, without warning, headlong into hospital life, with all of us sleeping in one small room; Marshall and Daddy in the hospital bed, me and a breastfeeding baby Kolby on a narrow pull-down bed. Doctors and nurses coming in at all hours; procedures in theatre, lumbar punctures, bloods, tests, chemotherapy, drugs – it was all-consuming and we weren't going home anytime soon.

A nurse popped her head around the door and asked if we wanted a cup of tea. "That sounds like the best offer I've had in a long time," I told her. Upon her return, she placed in front of me a cup of steaming hot tea. Not one of those small flimsy disposable cups where you have to be careful not to burn yourself, but a proper, big mug of strong tea. "I thought we weren't allowed open cups on the ward?" I asked her. "In situations like this," she replied, "there's only one thing that will do and that's a proper mug of tea" she winked as she left the room.

I sat staring at the tea, and my heart expanded to bursting. I could have hugged and kissed this woman. I felt such an extreme sense of gratitude for such a kind-hearted gesture, a gesture that had such an incredible impact on me, it's hard to find words to describe it.

I started practising 'extreme gratitude' wherever I could. Sick bowl already in the room? Extreme gratitude. Nurse makes Marshall laugh? Extreme gratitude. Play therapist available so I could shower? Extreme gratitude. The more I practised gratitude for the small things, the better things seemed to feel. And slowly, hour by hour, we started to navigate our new and unexpected life.

Months passed since Marshall's cancer diagnosis and I was desperate to have some time and space to myself. Ruth, the energy worker I knew, was running an 'Angelic Reiki Practitioner' weekend, but there was just no way I could get time away from the boys. Marshall's cancer treatment was still in full swing, Will was working full-time and I had both boys to care for, so I consigned it to the 'will revisit sometime in the future' shelf.

Time was passing and I was struggling more and more. I spoke to Will and said, "I'm going to have to push the 'big red button' if I don't get some help!" The 'big red button' was my code for saying things are getting super tough, and if nothing changes, I'll be having a breakdown because I just can't cope anymore. Thankfully, Will is my rock and the most amazing partner I could wish for, so he immediately arranged to take the boys to the grandparents. The afternoon was a flurry of packing what they needed to take… medications, chemo, thermometers, special nappies, creams, specific foods, supplements – everything!

As soon as they left and the door closed, I collapsed on the sofa and started mindlessly scrolling social media and there it was: Angelic Reiki Practitioner training starting at 7pm that evening... I rang Ruth. "You can join if you can be here in half an hour!" she said. "I'm on my way!" I replied.

So, without even knowing what I'd let myself in for, my adventure into realms I was previously unaware of began and I stepped into the world of energy healing. I practised grounding and protection. I discovered cleansing and attuning. I worked with chakras and meditation. I invited in spirit guides to work with me. I'd taken a chance on another life 'coincidence' and it turned out to be one of the most transformational weekends I could ever have imagined.

Alongside family life, the boys, caring for Marshall and his cancer treatment, the fire in my belly lit up when I started working with hypnotherapy clients. I launched my own business and spent every spare moment I had learning, training, and serving clients.

My journey led me back to Natasha, the woman I had initially spoken to that one morning when I was in the hospital with Kolby. She had developed the most incredible HeartHealing® methodology and I just knew I had to be part of it. I signed up to train with her and a year later, became one of the first-ever HeartHealing® practitioners in the world. I did sessions for friends, for clients, and soon I was being told over and over again "Cat you've found your thing!"

I didn't need to be told because I knew I'd found my soul purpose in life – empowering women to achieve more than they ever thought possible. I could feel it in my heart, my soul, my bones. Everything I was feeling was telling me 'Hell yes!' and now, I get to help clients all over the world fearlessly shine their brightest light; embodying their worth, evolving their intuition and expanding their capacity to receive more love, inner peace, and abundant success.

I always thought a 'spiritual awakening' was like a lightning bolt from the blue, and for some, it can be. For me, it has been more of a gradual series of consistent nudges and organic evolution; synchronicities that, when not ignored, have helped guide and unfold my life in the most incredible ways. Being spiritual doesn't mean that 'human' stuff doesn't happen to us – being human is one of the toughest gigs around! It's messy, tough, and totally unpredictable, but if we live with an open heart and follow the signs being shown to us, we can be divinely supported, no matter what is happening around us.

Our journey is never what happens to us but who we become in the process. Part of what creates our light is the experiences we have been through, the lessons of which we can share with others to help them traverse their own paths more lightly. It's only on reflection that I can see how the painful path, following my intuition and being guided by the 'coincidences' along the way, has brought me to living my purpose and being surrounded by the most incredible family I could wish for. I believe each and every one of us has an incredible, soul-led path within us, and it's our purpose in the world to follow what lights us up (literally!) and let that light out for the world to see.

As I write this, the door opens and I look at the six-year-old boy staring at me, the boy who can only have been a gift from the Universe. "Mummy, can I ask you a question?" he says. "Of course, always," I reply. "Mummy, is magic real?" I consider my answer: "Yes Marshall, I think it is. And so is the way you choose to see the world."

The GIFT Method™

The GIFT Method™ is a powerful tool I've developed for helping you navigate life and follow your path. GIFT stands for Gratitude; Intuition; F*ck Up; Take It and Trust.

Use it to guide you through your journey: to navigate daily life, the small steps and the big leaps. Use it when you're feeling stuck or need guidance.

GRATITUDE

Gratitude is a powerful energy-shifter. You will find gratitude not in the act itself, but in the energy that arrives in your heart. When we are able to allow ourselves to mindfully pause and to be in a state of gratitude for the smallest of things, it elevates the energy of us as individuals and those around us.

Find three small things each day to feel gratitude for; a green traffic light, the smile of a stranger, or a hot cup of tea! Think it to yourself, say it out loud, or write it down – it all counts!

INTUITION

We all have an incredible sense of intuition, which is there to support and guide us through our life's journey - you might know it as a gut feeling or just a sense that something feels 'right' or 'wrong'. It is perhaps one of the most powerful tools we have to guide us. Intuition is highly linked to trust, so the more you can heal any issues around trust, the more open to the power of your intuition you will be.

Trust yourself. Trust your insights, feelings, or any messages you might get – even when they make no logical sense. Listen. Follow the signs. You already know the answer.

F*CK UP (OR FAIL FORWARD IF YOU PREFER!)

Controlling life is not an option, it's an impossibility! We try and do it because we feel it keeps us safe, but in trying to control the outcome, we keep ourselves small and our light hidden. There are no mistakes in life, only lessons, and we get to choose to see that these are happening for us, not to us.

What if you couldn't fail? What if it was an impossibility to fail? How would life look and feel? What would you be doing differently?

TAKE IT & TRUST

Take the decision, the action, the next move. Be bold and heart-aligned. Show the Universe you are going after what you want and it will co-create the most beautiful outcomes with you. Do the 'next right thing' that feels aligned to you, and detach from the outcome. Trust that, even when you can't see it, everything is unfolding perfectly, just as it should.

What if you had unconditional trust in yourself? What if you had unconditional trust that everything was working for your highest good? How would life look and feel? What would you be doing differently?

MY FIVE KEY TAKEAWAYS

1. Use The Gift Method™ to guide you through life's journey – the small, every day steps and the big, life-changing leaps.
2. Ask yourself whether you're acting or reacting, from a place of love or fear. Love is the most powerful force available to us, live from it.
3. Healing the hidden wounds of your heart (we all have them) can be one of the greatest gifts you ever give yourself and those around you.
4. Guidance from the Universe may not make any sense to you at the time. That's OK! Logic can only take you so far.
5. Often gifts from the Universe arrive in a different way, in a different-shaped box to the one we were expecting. Keep an open mind and an open heart.

Dedication

To the women of the world who have the courage to heal their wounds, follow their hearts and forge their own unique paths. You are the change makers.

ABOUT THE AUTHOR

CAT MARSHALL

Cat Marshall is a Fearless Fairy Godmother to female entrepreneurs, helping them heal the hidden wounds of their heart to unlock their soul gifts, show up unapologetically, and effortlessly earn more.

Walking away from a settled personal life and career, Cat spent a decade breaking the mould of her own life and rebuilding it from scratch. Through startup business adventures and her own journey of personal growth, Cat finally found her true calling in healing, therapy, and coaching.

Cat loves motorcycling and has spent time touring the UK and Europe on her faithful Yamaha R6 'Bugsy'. When not child wrangling her two small boys, she can be found paddle-boarding on the stunning Pembrokeshire coastline where she lives.

Cat now helps women authentically shine their brightest light by embodying their worth, evolving their intuition, and expanding their capacity to receive, allowing them to create more than they ever thought possible.

Rise fearlessly with Cat's deeply transformational one-to-one sessions, or immerse yourself in one of her magical online programmes.

You can reach Cat at:

Email: hello@catmarshall.co

Website: www.catmarshall.co

facebook.com/catmarshallco
instagram.com/catmarshallco

5

MY FIRST OF MANY AWAKENINGS.

DONNA MARTIN

Right now, as my life stands, I live in the sheer beauty and truth of exactly who, and what, I am; a phenomenal spiritual being in a human body. What I love most about me is that I understand how powerful we really are as human beings and I have learned, through practice and persistence, how to live "The Good Life" now, while creating my dreams for tomorrow.

I am so proud of how far I have come on this journey, for my sheer courage and determination through it all, because I haven't always felt this way. But my burning desire for a better life has thankfully never let me quit. Now I have my amazing husband, Leego, and our three beautiful boys, Ollie, Leo, and Louie, to create my future with and I live in sheer gratitude for this every day.

Where it all began:

MY FIRST OF MANY AWAKENINGS.

My emotions and pain came at the tender age of just four and a half, on Christmas Eve when my mammy decided to walk out for good. The reason she gave was that she didn't love us anymore, or at least, that's what I believed she said all those years ago.

I remember looking at other families in our street, often wondering "why us?" What was it about us that was different? What had we done wrong?

It was the eighties, and back then, it was unheard of for women to leave their kids, it was usually the husbands that left. Our daddy was different, he stayed and raised five of us on his own, and we all got through it the best we could, with a bit of help from family and friends. We grew up in a place called Derry City, in Northern Ireland, which was renowned for its fighting and religious divide. But because my parents had been in a mixed religion marriage, religion was never ingrained in us like others. "Being a good Christian doesn't mean you have to go hugging the alter rails, Donna. It means treating others how you want to be treated yourself." That was my daddy's motto and it's stuck with me for life.

As a teenager, I went to mass almost every day. I recall the moment I overheard a neighbour gossiping about another neighbour behind their back, but, to their face, they were so friendly and nice. This felt confusing to me as it was ingrained in us to treat others respectfully and yet this person was doing the opposite. It had me questioning everything I was raised to believe in, so it was at this moment that I decided to stop going to mass. It didn't feel right for me anymore.

I looked at what others of my age around me were doing, and it wasn't long until I fell into the scenes of drink, drugs, and party times. I always felt, deep down, that I had a good moral compass inside, and my gut feeling was rarely wrong, but despite the warning signs I felt, I stayed on the road to self-destruct.

I went through phases of pity and self-doubt. I often asked myself, "why me?" I was always seeking others' approval, especially when it came to relationships. I searched for something or someone to fill the void, I felt inside. But no matter who or what came along, the void could never be filled. So, I continued to seek outside of myself, always longing for something more. I wasn't sure what that longing was, or even what it looked like anymore. I just knew that something felt missing, and I hadn't a clue how to fix it.

I went to a fortune teller when I was nineteen. He told me that I was destined for greatness, that I had a message to share with the world and I would be sharing on big stages, to audiences worldwide. Bear in mind, that I was working as a waitress at the time, with zero plan for my future other than my next night out. But somehow, the fortune tellers' words resonated deep within.

I continued to crash and burn fast. The feeling of not being worthy led me to constantly put myself down, get into bad situations and repeat this pattern consistently. I was frustrated at my actions, fed up with how I felt, and all I knew was that this time, something had to change. So, it did.

I believe the Universe/God/Spirit/Source, whatever you relate to, always has a better plan than the one we have for ourselves. So, when we can understand and learn how to step out of our own way, that's when we can truly let the power of the universe do its work. It's only when you look back and join the dots, that you get the full extent of the higher plans at play.

I look back on my life, and I would never have even dared to dream as big as the universe has provided to date. It was only when I began to understand this process that things really began to change for me. I was stuck at a crossroads in life and the universe showed me the way.

I started working as a home help for two amazing women, Kay and Margaret. Kay, in particular, saw something special in me. She used to comment that I would make a great nurse one day, and from those nurturing words, the seed was planted. Through their encouragement and support, I was able to borrow their belief and do what I needed to do to apply for my nursing degree. No one from my family had been to university, so this was important to me. Before meeting Kay and Margaret, university wasn't even on my radar. It was them that ignited a passion inside me I never even knew I possessed.

When I received a letter inviting me to a nursing interview, I was buzzing with adrenaline and excitement. I ran to Kay's house with the letter in hand, chuffed to bits at this news, beaming from ear to ear. They were both over the moon for me. I remember the smile on Kay's face. "See Donna, I knew you could do it. You're going to do amazing." Those words meant the world to me.

Three weeks later, she passed away. The loss I felt was immense. The only grief I had ever experienced up until this point was when my mum left all those years before. This brought up so many mixed emotions that I didn't feel equipped to deal with. It's only when you go through these experiences that you can truly look back and process, taking the strengths and learnings to grow and move forward.

A month later came interview time, and something strange happened. The day I went for the interview, I could feel a warm presence around my left side and, in an instant, I knew it was Kay. I didn't know how I knew, but I just knew. Every fibre of my being could feel the warm sense around me. It was like I had Spidey senses and they were off the chart, a warm soft blanket had surrounded me for protection, and that helped carry me through the interview.

I started my degree that September and sadly, in the November, my granny Francis died, and everything came crumbling down. My granny Francis was everything to me, especially after my mum left. Granny was the female role model and homemaker I looked up to, and this was a tough one to take.

All my doubts, worries, fears, and insecurities came flooding back, screaming at me to give up. Who did I think I was, going to university, thinking I could help people by becoming a nurse? I had the perfect excuse to quit, I had lost two important female role models in my life - my cheerleaders - in the space of 11 months, and things felt too much to cope with.

Within weeks of my granny's passing, I just couldn't seem to get it together. I was failing exams and seriously considering dropping out of university, and that's when things came to a head. You know, it's funny how the universe always guides you to exactly what you need, exactly when you need it.

My friend had suggested that I go to a spiritual healer who could also speak to the loved ones I had lost (the dead). In my head, I hadn't a clue about healing, spiritually or otherwise. I had learned, years before, to cry it out on my own in my bedroom, when no one else was around, then to paint on a smile and get on with it. But deep down, I was broken, and I knew it. All I wanted to know was that Kay's spirit was still with me, as mad as that may seem, as I knew it would give me so much comfort in a world where I felt lost. I also wanted to know that granny Francis was ok and that she was at peace with Kay. I was seeking comfort and solace... and I got much more than that.

That experience alone was a huge turning point for me. The woman confirmed straight away who Kay was and that yes, she was still there with me. She also confirmed about granny.

The most important takeaway for me was that I had been right all along. My gut instinct and feelings were right, I hadn't been going crazy. I could feel their spirits. Wow.... the sheer power and relief in this alone, was one of immense gratitude and love for what I was experiencing. I knew that things would never be the same again.

I cried a river of tears that day - tears of sadness, tears of joy, tears of relief. I felt like a massive weight had been lifted and things were going to change for the better. I had been right in using my Superpower of Intuition, but it's funny how it took a stranger to confirm what I'd already known in my heart of hearts.

Do you do that? Ask others opinions or advice when deep down, you already know your answer. How amazing would it feel to be able to tune in and trust yourself completely, 100,000%, without any shadow of a doubt, that you already have your answer within you? How would you like to have the confidence and self-belief in you to live your life this way? That is exactly how it feels and how I live my life now. It is also why I am so passionate about helping others to live this way too.

The Spiritual Healer gave me a powerful angel prayer that day and it is one that I use on repeat. It goes like this "Archangel Michael, Muriel, Gabriel, and Raphael, please tube me in your protective light for now and as long as I need it." (Repeat x 3 or as often as needed).

It has had such a phenomenal impact, not only on my life, but on all the people that I have passed it on to over the years, bringing great comfort, protection, and strength, exactly when it's needed. After this event, my awareness and curiosity for the angels and all things spiritual began to grow. The book "The Secret" was already out, and a spiritual awakening was happening all around me. More angel shops were opening in the town, crystals seemed to be the "in thing", along with incense and angel figurines, which I was rapidly collecting in abundance, along with the angel cards.

As I went deeper into it all, I thought I was becoming aware and flying high. I had just qualified as a registered nurse and landed my first permanent role in a leukaemia cancer ward. I was absolutely buzzing, high on life. I was spiritually good, talking to my angels daily, even consulting my angel numbers book (which I still use today) for the meanings and guidance of messages, doing my angel reading cards and getting a more consistent understanding of their messages.

I was making more money than I had ever made before, so I took the plunge at the height of the boom and went ahead and bought my first home, a beautiful two-bedroom flat. The first day I got the keys and moved in, I remember feeling so much pride for myself for all the things I had already been through and overcome. Little did I know, this was only the beginning.

I went to the cinema that evening with friends and when we came back, we drove up to find a group of over fifty youths gathered right outside my new home, having a massive street party. I couldn't believe what I was seeing and, to make matters worse, a girl was squatting, using my garden as a toilet. Mortified, I went straight inside, locked the door, and went to look out. The next thing, I saw a Budweiser bottle flying past. It crashed off my kitchen window, smashing the pane of glass.

What had I done!

I had a tremendous sinking feeling, right in the pit of my stomach. What was I going to do next? I rang the police, who politely told me, that the area I was living in was a no-go area. Sorry, what?

I had no idea there even was a no-go area. I knew it could be messy at times, but not to this extent, and the estate agent certainly didn't mention it. To make matters worse, I started questioning myself. I had gone to school in this area for years, I had friends that grew up here. Had I been so naive to think that I could live a happy life here? Or had I simply ignored warning signs before I bought? I hadn't a clue at this point. All I knew was that I thought I was spiritually connected, so how did I get this so wrong? I was so confused.

The party went on for hours, and I was up at 6 am for work. I had cried it out all night, cowered under the duvet, waiting to see what else they would break. I was hoping against all odds that this was simply a one-off. Surely, they now knew that someone was living here, so they would be polite enough to go somewhere else. No chance of that happening.

Instead, it became a regular thing, with youths gathering outside every day. Not as much as fifty, but usually between four and eight. I remember speaking to the youths, trying to plead my case. I thought if I explained to them that I was a nurse and was working in a cancer ward, they would understand, and things would improve. Unfortunately, it didn't. The more I confronted them, the more they wrecked.

I kept talking to my angels, trying to figure a way out, always asking for their guidance, to stay strong and positive, but things were starting to take their toll. Work was busy, and we were having a tough run with numerous patients, young and old, dying nearly every shift. I was living in a constant state of fear, playing all types of scenarios in my head, imagining the damage that might be done when I got home. I couldn't sit in my living room because it was upstairs and if the lights were on, the lads would blast the ball off the window, trying to get a rise. I wouldn't close the blinds because I wanted to keep an eye on what they were at. I felt like a crazy neighbour, living on my nerves. Something had to give.

One day, I had had enough. I lost it. My blood was boiling at this point. How dare they? This was my home, my life, they had no right to be here, and I told them so. This led me to receive my first-ever death threat. That changed everything!

I packed a bag and moved home to my daddy's. I left everything in the flat and continued to pay my mortgage. I couldn't see another way out. I felt physically and emotionally drained. I couldn't stop crying. I felt sick all the time and

I was constantly on edge. What the hell had happened to me? I used to think that I was so strong, so tough, but not now. I was a shell of my former self, and I couldn't keep it together anymore. I had to go off work on sick and everything came to a head.

I remember crying out to the angels and God, if there was one. Why me? Why again? Why not someone else? I couldn't, for the life of me, understand why this was happening to me. I thought that my mammy leaving was enough, that I had had my turn if you like. Have you ever done that? Rationalised or tried to portion out your so-called amount of pain to others? I thought I was awake to my spiritual side of things, so I should be good, right?

Now, you can call it what you want, but for me, this was when my divine intervention stepped in and steered me in the right direction. My cousin had just moved to Australia and told me to come for a break, to get my head right. I was that far gone, I had nothing to lose, and I needed to get out of Derry and far away from the nightmare of my life.

When the plane touched down in Australia, I felt like I could breathe for the first time (which reminds me of the Kelly Clarkson's song). The whole energy here was different, lighter, brighter somehow, and not just because of the sunny climate and warm weather. There was no heavy energy here. It's hard to explain, but when you feel like you've been living under a heavy cloud for so long, this change really hits you hard. It was like someone had lifted the lid off the box I was in, and now I was free to be me. To rediscover who I was after all this, where I was going, and what I needed to do next, without all the tears, heavy burdens, constant anxiety and stress. I felt able to smile for the first time in months without feeling guilty or like I was a fraud.

I spent a lot of time on the beach, reading the book, Eat, Pray, Love, by Elizabeth Gilbert and laughing to myself. Was this my road to recovery? Have you ever felt that much sadness inside, where you feel you're drowning and you can't get back up? I had been down for so long that I didn't even know if it was possible to come back; to be able to laugh again, for things to get better, for life to improve and for me to feel back to normal. I used to repeat to myself constantly

"I just want to feel happy."

Other people didn't understand. They just saw what they wanted to see. They couldn't know how I felt because they didn't have that experience. It was ok, it wasn't their fault, but I just wanted to feel "normal", whatever normal was. It's only now, all these years later, where mental health talks are more acceptable, that I can see just how many of us have been in a similar scenario, becoming prisoners in our own minds. Maybe you can relate to that, too.

I started thinking about the book's author Elizabeth, as this was based on her life, asking myself some questions. What did I really want? What did happy look like to me? I hadn't a clue. All I knew, was that I was ready to leave my pity party, I had been here for way too long. I felt like everyone had seen me as a victim. Was I going to be able to change? And if so, how was the happier me going to be? What was my new life going to look like? And what was I going to do about the flat?

I remember sitting down on the grass in Waverly Park, just off Bondi Road. It was another gorgeous day, and I was enjoying sitting in the shade, taking it all in. Kids were playing to my left and you could hear the hustle and bustle to the right from the traffic on the famous Bondi Road. I had been trying to figure out in my logical mind how I could get out of the position I was in with the flat, without having to go bankrupt.

Now, bear in mind, that I'd never had an overdraft or even a credit card. I had never been in debt because I was raised with the belief that if you didn't have the money to buy something, then you simply saved up for it first. So going bankrupt to me was horrific, a massive blemish against my name and, as silly as that may seem to some, it was where my belief was set, and it wasn't easy to change.

I was sitting on the grass having a conversation with God and the angels in my head. Going back and forth, bargaining like an idiot. I was trying to figure out how I could pay back my mortgage without "tarnishing" my name. I remember ringing daddy, back in Ireland, telling him how good it felt here, and daddy just said to me:

"It's time to be happy again, Donna. You need to move on with your life."

I put the phone down, lay flat on my back, and let the words sink in. Move on with my life!

How was I going to do that? Laying there, staring up at the beautiful sky, watching the clouds float by, I said to myself, "Right, if there is a god, if there are angels up there along with Kay and granny, now is the time to show yourself. I want a clear sign as to what I need to do next."

I half-heartedly offered it up, that if bankruptcy was my way out, then I'd better get a clear sign. At that moment, I began to get an overwhelming scent of roses. Which was strange, because I had been in the park a while and this smell wasn't there before. I remember looking around, but everyone had gone.

I just lay there, taking in the smell, because it brought me back to an event a few years earlier in Medjugorje, where I had come across a guest in our hotel that had collapsed and passed away the next day. But the strange thing was, I had been walking down the main street the day he died and got an overwhelming smell of roses and could sense that this person had just passed. I remembered I had stopped and looked at the time. It was 2.45 pm. Don't ask me how, but I knew he was gone. Fifteen minutes later, we got the call to confirm he had passed away, exactly at that time. Mind-blowing wasn't the word!

Suddenly, that feeling of knowingness washed over me again, this time with such strength, it was like my whole body was filling up with this powerful sheer bright light like I was levitating out of my body. All I could feel was pure love and strength, the warmth of the glow that took over me, and that smell of protection around me. The tears of gratitude came streaming down my face, and the feelings I felt were immense, nothing like I had ever felt before. And then I came back to life! That is the only way I can describe it.

My mentor, Bob Proctor, used to say that confidence is simply this, "It's when you know, and you know that you know with certainty" and that is exactly what happened to me that day. At that instant, I knew exactly what I had to do; it was time to file for bankruptcy. When I got home, I did exactly that. It was as if all the right people and resources came exactly at the right time, and I officially became bankrupt three months later.

I felt nervous leading up to the court date, as I didn't know exactly what to expect, and a lot of old fears and beliefs came up. But this time was different because I knew that God and the angels had a bigger plan for me and all I had to do was trust and hold the faith. I will never forget when the judge called my name, I could see him scanning through my file before he said:

"Donna, I'm sorry you've had to go through this, it clearly wasn't your fault. Now go and live your life, your free"

And just like that, all the debt was gone. All the worry, anxiety, and stress dispersed in an instant. Never, in my wildest dreams, could I have even made this up. This time, it was tears of joy, of relief running down my cheeks. I remember walking out of the courtroom and shrieking in delight, hugging my sister Sharan, in sheer amazement and disbelief. It was over. finished. And now it was time to move on!

My past has contained so many repeated lessons, that I wasn't always ready to learn, and it's only now through studying me, that I have been able to process and see the steps needed to let go, move on and be free!

I have learned the tools needed to step into my truth, the greatness we all have within, and it's through these powerful processes that I have stepped into the real authentic me! No longer a victim of circumstance, I have re-emerged stronger, happier, confident, and free. Living my life in the truth of why I am here and helping others to live their truth too.

I proudly live my adult life today with my husband and three amazing boys. I am filled with love, gratitude, happiness, and contentment, living from my inside/out. I no longer feel that emptiness within. It is gone, it's done, and I am free by loving me!

It's not always going to be easy, especially at the beginning of your journey, because we have been so conditioned and programmed to live our life, seeing the world through our eyes and our senses, instead of through our powerful imagination. But by re-educating ourselves and understanding that we really are the creators of our world, we can then become disciplined and focused on the outcomes we really want, instead of staying focused on the things that we don't want, which is how most of us currently live today.

Every day, I can dip into my "Toolbox 22" and apply multiple learned skills and routines for successfully living in alignment with my mind, body, and soul.

I believe that awareness and knowledge are key in opening your reality to the power and possibilities of this physical world, and I am now passionate about serving others through my business, "The Goodlife 22", where, as a Mindset Results Coach, I teach individuals that are stuck or at a crossroads in life ,how to face their fears, grow their confidence and live their Goodlife too.

Thank you for taking the time to read this part of my journey and the start of my many awakenings. In the future, I look forward to sharing with you some more of my amazing experiences, where the universe has had my back, in bigger and better ways than I ever could have imagined. But for now, I hope that my experiences have inspired and motivated you to have a look at where you're at, because it really is, never too late to change.

All you need to do is make the decision and take guided action. Remember that your intuition will steer you in the right direction, to your own true purpose in life.

So, when you decide to start living your life, your way, on your terms, in alignment with the Universal Laws, you will begin to find that the right people, resources and circumstances will always show up when you need them.

P.S. Remember, it takes no more energy to think good, positive, empowering thoughts, creating the reality you want, than it does to think poor, negative, draining thoughts to create the one that you don't.

It's up to you. We all have the power to choose. I choose to live "The Goodlife "every day, and I hope that I have inspired you to do this too.

Lots of Love Donna x

MY FIVE KEY TAKEAWAYS

Take these amazing tools and add them to your daily toolbox.

1. Always trust your intuition (that initial gut feeling inside). Its only job is to protect you and steer you in the right direction.
2. When the Sh... does hit the fan, choose faith over fear and trust that the Universe has a better plan.
3. Love yourself enough to put yourself first! When you're ok, it automatically has a ripple effect out to those you love.
4. Repeat the Angel Prayer for protection as often as you need it. Archangel Michael, Muriel, Gabriel, and Raphael, please tube me in your protective light for now and as long as I need it.

5. Simply ask yourself every day, am I doing what I love to do? And remember, it's NEVER too late to start again.

In order for change, **you** must change...

Dedication

I dedicate this chapter to my inner child, for never giving up on me. For my willingness to let go and let God and the angels lead the way through my spiritual awakening, and to my amazing sister, Sharan, for being by my side through it all.

Thank you, I love you, sis. xxx

ABOUT THE AUTHOR

DONNA MARTIN

Donna Martin is a Mindset Results Coach who passionately mentors her clients through the internationally successful program "Thinking into Results ". Donna starts to engage her clients' minds at both the conscious and unconscious level right from the very first session, often getting immediate breakthroughs. Donnas unique style of coaching enables her clients to actively update their internal programming to one of happiness, freedom, confidence, and self-belief.

Before starting her supportive Facebook community, The Goodlife 22, Donna spent over 15 years as a nurse. Her vast experience from this position made the transition into full-time coaching a natural progression. In her role as a Coach, a light worker and a phenomenal leader Donna thrives on giving service to those ready to Awaken, showing them how to take their life to the next level and live their Goodlife too.

Donna loves to spend her days challenging her husband and three boys to think creatively, while having fun along the way. She is constantly pushing them and herself out of their comfort zones. While she also loves to bring out her dancing diva every now and again with old skool dance tunes and RnB classics from the 90s.

Donna is available for one-to-one coaching, as an engaging leader for group coaching, and expert speaker at public and private corporate mindset events.

She can be found on:

www.facebook.com/groups/thegoodlife22

 facebook.com/thegoodlife22donnamartin
 instagram.com/thegoodlife22donnamartin
 linkedin.com/in/thegoodlife22donnamartin

6

BREAKING THE SILENCE: MY HORMONES, MY PURPOSE

ELISSA DOBSON

" **To regret the past is to forfeit the future.** "

This is an old Chinese Proverb that one day, I plan to get tattooed on the inside of my arm so I can see it whenever I need to be reminded to stop looking backwards and keep pushing forwards. I can't remember when I first heard the proverb but over the past few years, it has taken on a new meaning, and I can honestly say I now live my life by it!

Today, as I write this, I am proud to say I am living my most authentic life. I'm many things, such as a mum, wife, daughter, sister, business owner, and survivor of life, but the thing I'm most proud of is: I'm ME.

In the past few years I've discovered my life's mission and, at the age of 50, I'm embracing a new chapter of my life's journey, and not allowing any of the setbacks I've experienced to determine my worth.

My awakening was the moment I acknowledged and embraced the power of my hormonal menopausal journey and how it has shaped my mind, body and spirit connection.

That was the day I realised I could be the person I chose to be rather than the person others expected me to be. It was the day that allowed me to move forward with focus, positivity and enabled me to release the regret from past choices and experiences.

I am proud to now help professional women blindsided by menopause to understand their own hormonal journey so they can take control and get their life and career back on track.

As a Menopause, Mindset, and Leadership Coach, I work with individuals and businesses to understand and overcome the impact that something as natural as menopause can have on our physical, psychological, and behavioural health (and, dare I say it, our spiritual identity!)

This is definitely the purpose of my life now and in the future, but has not always been my past.

WHO IS 'SHE'?

I have learnt to recognise that we need to constantly work to balance the three essential elements of self, which I believe are:

our mind (thoughts);

our bodies (hormones); and

our spirit ('she').

Although I wouldn't describe myself as a spiritual person, I have always been a free spirit. I resonate with the fact that we each have a deeper spirit, but it is sometimes easy to push 'her' down. To stop listening to 'her'. To let logic and circumstance take over. To forget what the point of our life is.

I believe we have a spirit and a soul, which I describe as 'she' or 'her', as 'she' is an integral part of my identity. Over the years, I have learnt to tune in to 'her' and 'listen' to when I am not being authentic to my purpose; or hear 'her' celebrate when I've followed my heart, even when logic is telling me to stop!

Whether you personally describe it as your gut feeling, a higher being, or your sense of intuition, I'm certain we all can focus in on our deeper selves. It does not always come easily, but 'she' is always there.

At points during my life, I've been described as an 'ice queen' and a 'hard-faced bitch'. Neither persona would give an insight into the deep, inner turmoil that I've carried for much of my life: the lack of confidence in myself, the uncertainty of my value in the world, the total feeling of being an imposter in my own life.

On reflection, I, like many people, had built up thick walls around my deeper, inner self, for self-preservation and simply because it is easier to hide your true self than to be honest and explore who 'she' really is. I grew up thinking that to be spiritual meant you had to be religious. I thought to believe in a higher self, meant believing in a version of God. I assumed that to say 'I love myself' meant I was a selfish or uncaring person.

For so much of my life, I've lived by the labels or job titles I thought I needed, to ensure I fit into society, to improve my career development, and fit the 'norm'. I now wonder, what the hell normal is anyway?

Today, I can truly say I have embraced the label of 'Elissa'. I am happy to be me and although at times, I still have feelings of not being good enough, or questioning my purpose, I have learnt that these are natural thoughts that nearly everyone has, and the most powerful gift I have is to be authentically me.

If I could speak to the 18-year-old Elissa, I would remind her that she is beautiful, inside and out. She should not give value to the negative words from other people or allow them to steer her life. It is OK to be spirited and questioning. It is OK not to have all the answers. It is OK to follow your heart, listen to your head and be driven by your hormones, particularly when you know it aligns with your inner purpose. It is OK to make mistakes and move on, without believing you have failed or let yourself or others down. It is OK to discover who Elissa is, because she has the answers within 'her'.

CHILDHOOD IN PARADISE...

Let me take you back to my childhood, out in the country-side of New South Wales (NSW), Australia. I am the third of three kids and, along with my parents, we spent years circumnavigating the globe. From the time I was born to my mid-twenties, we had moved from Australia to the UK and back multiple times, until I made the UK my permanent home at the age of 25. I think we had lived in over a dozen houses before I was in my teens (enough to unsettle anyone, let alone a child).

My parents are both strong and incredible characters, but in hindsight, they were not a perfect match as a couple and throughout my childhood, they spent many years separating and getting back together, 'for the good of the children', until they eventually amicably divorced in their eighties!

As children, we are born with an instinct to be inquisitive, accepting, and open to all that is around us, however, our experiences leave traces of hurt and trauma that can erode our free spirit and lead us into thoughts and beliefs that our mind interprets into truth. As a child, nobody ever said to me 'you are not good enough', however, my mind created this belief, and it grew in strength for years to come. I felt I'd done something that led to my parents' ongoing disagreements, constant house moves, and breakdown of our family structure.

NEW TOWN, NEW ME?

When I was 13, my parents were living apart, my sister had left home, and it was just mum, my brother, and me. We moved from the countryside in NSW to near Sydney at the start of my second year of high school. I suddenly had to settle into a new town and new school where I knew no one. Starting a new school is challenging at the best of times, but in your formative, hormonal teenage years, it is incredibly hard.

I soon learnt that to 'fit in', I needed to dumb down, wear the right shoes, shorten my skirt, and do just enough to get by in lessons, because then I was accepted into a peer group. Don't get me wrong, I made some great friends, but the lessons I learnt was 'don't be an individual because then you become a target for others.

At times, when I was sobbing about the unfairness of life, 'she' would try to shout, "you are strong, brave, and enough", but the pain and hurt I was feeling would smother and drown out her words. With my mum working long days and nights as a nurse, I had enough freedom to push the boundaries until at 16, my focus slipped to the allure of drink, drugs, and boys.

HAPPILY EVER AFTER... AT 18?

So, fast forward to a few days before my 19th birthday, and I was walking down the aisle to marry my boyfriend of only a few years. I had only finished high school a few weeks before and, despite everyone trying to talk me out of my decision to get married, I was convinced that I was making the right decision. He wasn't the first boy I kissed, but he was the first boy to promise me a lifetime of happiness and security, something I felt I'd been missing due to the episodes of separation of my parents, the constant moves, and the crumbling of our family unit.

Could I honestly say I was in love? I don't think I could say it then, and I certainly recognise now that this wasn't a love match. It was a security blanket that I believed would provide me with refuge and stability to move forward into my adult years. Did I hear 'her' scream "Don't do it!" at me on the morning of my wedding? Yes, but I pushed down my doubt and on went the wedding dress, flowers in my hair, and tentative smile.

In essence, I swapped one label for another. I'd been a 'daughter' and was now a 'wife'. I dropped my dreams of going to university and instead worked full-time in an office, commuting three hours a day, and paying a mortgage on a house that was far too much of a burden for a young couple.

Whilst my friends were out partying and exploring the world, I was feeling shackled to a relationship that didn't supply my emotional needs. The reality of marriage, mortgage, and mundane work did nothing for my spirit. I felt trapped and isolated, and was reminded that my voice was no longer my own. If my husband or his parents decided, for instance, what house to buy or what car we drove, I was expected to go along with it, despite my uncertainty or unhappiness.

Communication, fairness, and having a voice, I discovered, was not part of the picture for our betrothal. My spirit was pushed ever further down.

NEW BABY, NEW JOY...

The greatest gift that this marriage gave me was my amazing daughter, Karla, who was born when I was 24. She brought purpose into my life. However, the joy I was expecting to feel was dampened by severe postnatal depression, which was described at the time as me having 'the wobbles', rather than having a valid hormonal imbalance and quite serious mental health issue.

I remember an appointment with a male doctor, where I was sobbing, asking for help, and I was told the best thing to do was to get on with looking after my baby. There was no mention of looking after myself! At the time, I believed I was a failure and thought my daughter would be better off with anyone other than me. My vision of the future was grey. I couldn't see beyond each day and knew my life, and the life I was giving my daughter, was not what I wanted, but I thought I just needed to carry on. As the saying goes, "I'd made my bed and needed to lie in it".

Oh, how I wish I could go back now and give the younger version of myself a hug and tell her it was going to be OK!

UK, THE LAND OF HOPE

About five years after our marriage, my parents had reconciled once again and returned to live in the UK. After trying to 'get on with it', look after my baby daughter, deal with undiagnosed postnatal depression and manage the relationship with my husband, which had become unbearable, I finally recognised that if nothing changed, nothing would change.

I remember a tearful phone call with my mother, where I admitted I needed her help. Our relationship at this point had become tenuous, not due to a lack of love, but due to my inability to ask for help. In hindsight, I recognise that this is a classic trauma response, due to the belief that I had been the reason for much of the upset within the family.

Once I'd expressed my desire to leave the situation I was in, the wheels were set in motion and on 6th May 1996, I arrived in the UK after a 24-hour flight with a suitcase and my baby. To paraphrase the lyrics of Alanis Morissette's song, "All I Really Want", was 'some peace now'. I was traumatised and terrified of what lay ahead, but I was acting on the overarching instinct of the need to protect the most precious thing in my life, my daughter. To do that, I recognised I needed help, support, and love.

Despite speaking the same language, the north Cheshire town of Macclesfield where my parents lived, was totally foreign. It was cold, even in the middle of summer. It had small roads and even smaller houses. I was a stranger in a foreign land, but I realised quickly I was safe.

When people, inevitably asked me, "So when are you going back home? You must miss Australia?", I'd stare at them blankly for a few seconds and wonder "where is home?" Was it back in 'the land of plenty', my marital house with a husband who was now a stranger and a life that was suffocating? Or was it in this new town on the other side of the world, where I felt I had a clean slate and an opportunity to find myself? A chance to build an unknown future but one that I had control of?

Both options were equally frightening, but then I had a lightbulb realisation: I could be anyone I wanted to be. Without the shackles of my previous life, I was able to breathe and I started to realise I had the ability to love and be loved without question!

For the first time in my adult life, I spoke to a counsellor and realised that I wasn't to blame. I recognised my journey up to this point had been controlled by a combination of hormones - as a child, teenager, and adult - as well as the physical and emotional experiences I had lived through. I began to see that I was in control of my own destiny and the universe had transpired to lead me to a new life in the UK.

Following the finalisation of my divorce, I bought my own house, doted on my amazing daughter, settled into a new career, and met the love of my life and now husband of nearly 20 years, Chris.

LOVE AND LOSS

After a gorgeous summer wedding celebration, where my mum and daughter walked me down the aisle, Chris and I decided to try for a baby. We were blessed to conceive quickly and were excited to be expecting our new daughter. Unfortunately, at the same time I was informed out of the blue that my role was being made redundant at the company I'd worked at for several years. A few weeks later, we lost our daughter due to complications and my life was rocked once again.

I no longer had the joy of looking forward to our much-wanted daughter, I no longer had a job, and my resolve in life was once again smashed. The pain I felt was heart stopping, but the difference was, I had a partner who loved me, an extended family who supported me and a deeper belief that things happen for a reason.

I had been exploring the world of spirituality, of looking beyond the obvious and researching the mind, body, and spirit connection. Through a combination of books, local events, and new friends I was opening my mind to the existence of 'her' within me. I knew I didn't have all the answers, however, I was beginning to embrace the power of intuition and a greater purpose.

FROM THE TOP OF THE MOUNTAIN TO BOTTOM...

Despite the rollercoaster of emotions, I kept putting one foot in front of the other and soon we were blessed to welcome our incredible son, Charlie, into the world. At the same time, I started a new career where I was mentored by an amazing female boss, who always saw the potential within me, and encouraged (occasionally pushing) me to step out of my comfort zone to develop my skills, abilities and confidence.

As a valued senior manager, I learnt that I loved managing and coaching people, helping them to set their sights on the top of their own mountain and support them to achieve what they set out to do. In turn, their success became the success of the business. Despite inevitable changes to our management structure, the common-place politics, and the upsets that run through most large businesses, I always strived to turn up with a positive attitude and give 100% of myself. I believed my career was safe and secure.

Unfortunately, after nearly a decade in the organisation and heading into my mid 40s, I was faced with a culmination of issues. I had a new boss and, although female, that is where the similarities to my previous boss ended. From my perspective, her focus was on spreadsheets and statistics, rather than people and opportunities. I think it is sufficient to say that our opinions differed on most aspects of running the business.

I was also struggling with concentration, confidence, and a feeling of lack of control over my life. I was unable to remember simple things, like the names of people I'd worked with for years. I would get the feeling of complete overwhelm when I had to make decisions, or experience an unwanted, emotional shedding of tears in the middle of a meeting.

I knew something wasn't right but couldn't put my finger on it. Following a visit to the doctor, I came out with a prescription for anti-depressants and recommendation to manage my stress. Although the tablets brought some benefit, I was still sliding down a slope that I didn't understand and couldn't stop.

THE BREAK(DOWN)

After months of struggling with both my mental and physical health, plus the ongoing battle with my boss, who I perceived was slowly stripping away my authority and purpose, I reached breaking point.

It was a Friday evening; I was sat in my office finishing some work off. Everyone had left to enjoy their weekend, except for my boss. She came in and her presence blocked the doorway. I honestly can't remember exactly what she was saying but it felt like a barrage of anger and negativity. I interpreted from her words how awful she thought I was; how I needed to be better and do better.

I felt trapped. I was physically shaking, felt bile rise up my throat, was holding my head in hands watching the tears falling from my eyes and pooling on the desk below me. I felt myself break apart. I was empty and at the complete mercy of another person. I didn't have the energy to lift my head, to argue back, to protect myself or to tell myself it was OK. It wasn't OK. I wasn't OK.

I couldn't stop the feeling that my spirit had finally left me. After 10 years in a job surrounded by friendships, success and security, I grabbed my bag and walked out of the building. Never to return.

NEXT STEPS...

After the initial shock of that life-changing action, I vowed I would never give the control of my life over to another person. I vowed I never wanted to be employed again. I knew that by walking out, I had, in some way, taken control of my life.

I was suddenly faced with a blank sheet of paper – what to do next? My mental health was in tatters but my kids needed me, my husband needed me, and I had been given a new path which was still unseen but offered hope and opportunity.

So, at the age of 47, rather than following the obvious path of getting another full-time 'safe' job, I decided to try something I'd always harboured a desire to do. I went about setting up my own business! I reviewed my skills and decided I could be a Virtual Assistant.

I registered a company name, undertook an in-depth course on how to run a business, and threw myself into the world of business networking. I was blown away with how virtual strangers would become my cheerleaders and value the skills I offered.

I had people who would introduce me to their connections and say "You must meet Elissa; she is incredible and can definitely help your business". I was invited to give presentations about ways of communicating and coaching staff. My stories of overcoming adversity were welcomed as inspirational and motivational.

I felt valued and my sense of purpose to help others was reignited. The world of self-development and continual learning was presented to me as a positive opportunity that I could absorb with energy and focus. I was encouraged by those around me that it was absolutely fine to be ambitious but kind and genuine at the same time. I developed greater self-awareness and went on to study Neuro-Linguistic Programming (NLP), Mental Health First Aid, and coaching skills.

TIME TO BE HONEST

Despite my initial success, I recognised I was still not fulfilled or living authentically. After working with an amazing life coach, I understood I needed to release the hurt I was still holding onto from the trauma of leaving my corporate job. Until I did this, I would never truly be whole.

The start of my powerful awakening journey was learning to slow my mind, to focus on simple breathing techniques, and to look in a mirror and say 'I love you' with authenticity and belief. I understood that other people's opinions of me should not dictate my life. I finally had the tools to start hearing 'her' again. My guiding light, my spirit, and my soul. She had never left me. I just hadn't been listening!

I welcomed spending hours journaling and thinking about my WHY. How could I be honest with other people if I wasn't being honest with myself? Up until this point in my life I had never considered writing down my WHY. This is what I wrote:

> *To do something that I feel passionate about every day, which creates emotional balance and happiness within me. To live authentically, with self-love, respect, and belief. To provide financial security and a loving and safe*

*environment for my family. To have choice in the decisions
I make."*

My WHY was no longer focused on the label of who I
thought I was, or the restrictions of someone else's expectations. I had allowed my deeper self to be heard and imagine
a life led by joy and purpose.

Before I could embrace this new chapter, I made a conscious
effort to hold my hand on my heart and say "thank you" to
my previous boss for setting me on this journey. If I had not
been steered to take control and leave my 9 to 5 corporate
existence, I would not have had this incredible opportunity
to design my life, my why and my future.

I consciously released the hurt and anger I was carrying and
opened myself to a future of possibilities and growth. I
began feeling lighter. The knot in my shoulders released and
my smile returned! I was stepping into the true embodiment
of 'Elissa' for the first time since I could remember.

HAVING HORMONES, OR A LACK OF THEM

During this journey of discovery, I realised that my
hormones had been playing a silent but significant game
with me for many years.

Little did I know that the cause of my struggles with confidence, concentration, and control during the period of me
walking out of my job was not down to a 'mental break-

down'. I was, in fact, perimenopausal, and my hormones were going through a natural yet significant yo-yoing that affected my whole being. I wasn't losing my mind; I was losing hormones!

Although I understood that the menopause journey was a natural transition that every woman on the planet would face, I wasn't aware that the symptoms, effects, and age of onset, could all vary significantly, with very real impacts on women's psychological, emotional, and physical wellbeing. I discovered that in the UK, nearly a third of a million women every year leave their jobs because of the effects of menopause. I recognised I wasn't on my own; I'd become one of the statistics.

I knew I could no longer be silent. In the middle of the night, 'she' was whispering to me, to be part of the change for womanhood worldwide. I had complete belief that I could make a difference, to be part of the solution. I had overwhelming clarity that my mission was to engage, educate, and empower the world about the impact of menopause in the workplace.

By stepping up and sharing my experience, I could help break the taboo and give power to others to embrace this empowering chapter of a woman's life, without fear or uncertainty. This was my purpose!

MISSION MENOPAUSE WAS BORN

With a new burning passion, I undertook an intensive Executive Menopause Coaching course, met my future business partner and like-minded menopause warrior, Caroline, and we launched our business, Mission Menopause.

Our focus is to educate individuals and the business world about the menopause journey, why women may struggle, and how best to support them. We share our experiences of how, with improved awareness, all women can learn to navigate their own journey, whether it is through tailored adjustments and better support in the workplace, assistance from the healthcare profession, or simply by sharing their concerns in a safe and welcoming space.

The shout for a menopause revolution is loud and comes from many directions. It is not coming just from women, as many men want to better understand how to recognise and support their female partners and colleagues through this, often misunderstood, transition as well.

With support and empathy, people in the workplace should feel engaged with being part of the menopause conversation; be educated about the impact of our hormones (or lack of them); given the tools and confidence to make work a safe haven for all; be empowered to make change happen and embrace all that menopause brings.

WOMEN SUPPORTING WOMEN

The need to find my own safe support network and access to easily available, evidence-based information led me to help set up a local menopause support group. It was in this secure environment that women voiced their own struggles and questions. Being able to share 'is hair loss a thing?' or 'where has my libido gone?', was empowering and eye-opening.

Women from all walks of life came together and said "thank goodness the conversation has started, I thought I was on my own." By coming together, we could inspire positive action for individuals and the community as a whole.

YOU'RE AN INSPIRATION!

Imagine my surprise when out shopping recently, an old colleague came up to me, threw her arms around my shoulders and said, "Thank you for what you are doing, you're an inspiration to me!" I was taken aback but quickly realised that despite her outward confidence, her world had been rocked by those pesky hormones.

Unbeknown to me, she had been 'lurking' on social media and following my journey, which had enabled her to take control of her own life and in turn, her family dynamics. She shared that despite her marriage being rock solid for years, her relationship with her husband had recently become strained and on the verge of breaking down.

Once she'd recognised that her mood swings and unexplained rages were related to perimenopause, with the help of HRT and honest communication with her partner, her relationship was stronger than it had been in years!

This experience showed me that when women support each other with love and honesty, we can all dig deeper, discover our authentic selves and create positive change.

BREAKING THE SILENCE

I look back and wonder how different things would have been if I'd known then what I know now, however, even as I write this, I feel a deep sense of gratitude for the journey I've travelled. I know that the painful experiences I went through were the ones which gave me the greatest gifts, even if I couldn't see it at the time; gifts that have allowed me to find a new, spirit-led path, and uncover my true authentic self.

One of the most powerful things that I heard was "you're not losing your mind; you're losing your hormones." Whether it is the teenage transition, changing post-partum hormones or Menopause they are natural stages for a woman's body to transition through, and I'm a strong believer that by sharing our experiences, by bringing communities together, and by breaking the silence that so often surrounds these natural stage in life, we can transform the lives of both ourselves and others.

I wish someone had told me that the effects of hormones through the years are normal and that we can choose to see menopause as the gateway to a new chapter of our lives. It is the moment where we can step into our 'wise woman', and take great learning from our experiences - the good and the bad; as an opportunity to open ourselves up and embody our truest selves. It is a time to stand up, smile and shout "I am proud to be me!"

My hope for you is that you find your own journey of mind, body and spirit connection. That you slow down and start listening to 'her' and learn to love and believe in yourself deeply, and to live by your 'WHY'.

You have the power to be the change in your world and the world around you, even if you can't see the whole world in one step. Have faith, take that first step and the rest will follow.

I find myself smiling now, as I know 'she' is proud.

MY FIVE KEY TAKEAWAYS

1. Send love to your younger self and tell her how amazing and strong she was. Tell her what she needed to hear. There are no mistakes in life, only lessons to be learnt to help you move forward.
2. Release the negative. Make space in your soul for love and positivity by freeing those unhelpful and

heavy negative emotions. Make your own journey of healing and emotional wellbeing a priority.

3. Tune into 'her'. Find a safe space, gift yourself quiet time, breathe consciously and deeply, and be still. Tune into messages, thoughts, and feelings that come up from your spirit, your soul. 'She' is with you always.

4. Embrace change – whether it is circumstantial, environmental, or hormonal. Change is inevitable and when you embrace it with power and understanding, amazing things can happen.

5. Give gratitude, kindness, and love to your mind, body and spirit, for all that it has been through and all that it is going through. You are amazing!

Dedication

I dedicate this chapter to the three women of wisdom in my life: My mother, Thelma; my sister, Jane; and my daughter, Karla. You have taught me how to love, live, and laugh.

ABOUT THE AUTHOR

ELISSA DOBSON

Elissa Dobson is the Co-Founder of Mission Menopause and is a qualified and accredited Executive Menopause Coach. She specialises in menopause, mindset, and leadership coaching for women leaders and organisations who want to become menopause friendly.

Following a 20-year career in Healthcare Management, including seven years as a non-clinical Operating Theatre Manager, Elissa was devastated when she joined the 10% of working women in the UK who leave their careers due to the effects of menopause.

Following the shock of leaving her job, Elissa was determined to become part of the positive change for women everywhere. Now, using her experience and expertise, Elissa brings the topic of menopause to life and is passionate about creating open and safe conversations that leave people feeling engaged, educated, and empowered.

Elissa specialises in delivering interactive workshops, one-to-one leadership coaching, motivational talks, educational webinars, and strategic consultancy that, in turn, benefit her clients with improved recruitment, retention, employee well-being, and organisational reputation.

Whether enjoying a walk in the local Peak District with her faithful dog Sasha or catching up over a beer and BBQ, Elissa loves spending time with family and friends and has never lost her unique Australian sense of humour!

Elissa offers group mastermind programmes and one-to-one coaching sessions for professional women, whose career, confidence, or capabilities are being affected by their hormonal journey, and organisations who want to become menopause friendly.

You can reach Elissa at:

Email – hello@missiomenopause.com

Website - www.missionmenopause.com

linkedin.com/in/elissa-dobson

7

CHASING THE UNKNOWN

LAURE POLIDORI

Here I am, on my terrace, typing on my laptop in the shade on a sunny afternoon. I feel excited about typing these words that are getting me closer to my dream of being a published author. Content and calm, I am where I am supposed to be, at least for the time being.

I enjoy living in the mountains, with a view over the sea. Every day, I wake up to the sound of birds chirping. I enjoy my daily morning walks with my dog, after which, I take some time to sip my soya latte, enjoying the view over the green and blue of nature with the buzzing bee's soundtrack in the background. I choose who I work for and with, as well as the amount of work I am willing to take on. Most importantly, I don't start working before 10 am, a luxury I remind myself to savour every day.

When I was little, I used to listen to a song in French, which highlighted how impossible it was for someone to enjoy a sunny Monday due to the fact it is a working day. This really stuck with me, almost like an unconscious goal. I used to dread Monday, it meant the start of five days of "musts" and "have to's", back to crowded tubes, buses being delayed and the uncertainty of what time I might get home at the end of the day due to the high possibility of trains being cancelled last minute.

I'd invite everyone to pause and think about it. How do you feel about Mondays? It used to take me forever to wake up and get out of bed. I would keep on snoozing the three different alarms set on my phone, delaying getting up as much as possible, particularly during London's winter, with the shortage of daylight and overcrowded tubes. Just the thought of it would drain and frustrate me, as well as make me lazy. I was a bit like a car that struggles to get started on a cold winter morning.

Things are entirely different now. I do enjoy Mondays. In fact, this is the day I work the fewest hours, ensuring I enjoy my afternoons by focusing on myself; by taking golf lessons, something I've wanted to do for a while now; or by treating myself to a coffee catch-up with a friend, then going grocery shopping - supermarkets tend to be empty on that day of the week. So yes, most of my Mondays feel sunny now!

I am proud to say I have moved on from toxic relation-ships, both personal and professional ones. I now have some grounded boundaries in place and ensure I put myself first. I speak up when something does not sit well with me. I feel much calmer, happier, and healthier.

One big indicator of the above is that my need for travelling has dissipated. Anyone who knows me well would be astounded to hear me say that I do not feel the need for travelling anymore. And yes, that's the truth. Of course, it would be nice to get on a long-haul plane, I do enjoy those long trips where you are being fed and your only worry is to decide which movie you are going to watch, but no longer am I desperate to get on a plane and fly to the other side of the planet. Bottom line, I am finally happy to be home. Home within myself. This brings up a gratifying feeling as I think about how I finally got to this point because it's taken me many years of trying to find where I feel I belong.

Not so long ago, I would spend my time working and trying to convince someone to go on a trip to the other side of the world to visit new places which, deep down, I was hoping I would fall in love with and feel happy in. I was expecting some kind of epiphany that would say "This is your happy place; you must move here". I was on a quest to find my "happy place", one I would feel immersed in, with a 24/7 smile on my face, worry-free, and always having a positive outlook on life. A true happy-go-lucky feeling. I would look for something new every chance I had.

The reality is, I didn't really know what I was looking for, except for that feeling of happiness.

I used to pour all my energy into thinking about what I didn't have. I was focusing on the family ties I didn't have, the intimate relationships I seemed unable to maintain, how my loved ones were so far away, the disconnection with friends, the time I didn't have to take on some class, or the lack of money to buy a metallic blue convertible Audi S3, or me not being able to have a dog.

I would fixate on what I thought was missing from my life, only the more I focused on what I didn't have, the more unattainable it would feel. I recognised I was too negative a person to be around, but the challenge wasn't the awareness, it was not knowing what to do about it. I rarely smiled, let alone laughed and I would wake up in the morning as if I was on autopilot, with no purpose or excitement. I felt lonely.

I reached a point where I was surprised by those who were still around, checking on me, putting up with me, and equally, I would be disappointed by those who weren't. I used to think I was born in the wrong era, one in which falseness, sell-out, and hypocrisy prevailed over loyalty, honesty, friendship, and companionship.

I was living in fear of being alone and haunted by the idea of becoming homeless, of not being able to take care of myself, of losing the little I had, of never reaching the point of making my dreams come true. In hindsight, I don't even think I really knew what I wanted. I felt no one would ever value me for who I was and what I had to offer. I suppose that's what you get when you reach a point where you don't value yourself. I knew, deep down, I was worthy of love, but thought that I was never at the right place or time.

Of course, these sensations were not present every day of the year, there were times I would go on holiday or enjoy a particular event where I would feel alive and happy, and I would smile and laugh. Life is kind and gave me something to truly enjoy every now and then, but it would never last.

One thing I wish I could tell my younger self: Stop searching outside and start looking inside, that's where your true home is. I would tell myself to let go of expectations, learn to appreciate what I do have and trust the universe will provide. After all, challenging times are needed, they are the ones that help you grow. You just have to trust that things will get better eventually.

The real deep challenge was that I felt I didn't belong anywhere. From my earliest years, I moved many times, not only to different cities, but even to different countries, so, wherever I would go, I'd feel different.

I remember one day in class, the teacher asked us to read out loud one after the other, and when it came to my turn, she made fun of me in front of the whole class because I had a southern accent. You can imagine the impact this has on a nine-year-old, and how it aggravated the feeling of being different. Thinking about it today, I wonder if that's the

reason I have always done my best to get the best pronuncia-
tion I can when learning a new language, but at that time, it
certainly didn't feel positive.

For as long as I can remember, although I didn't have the
words for it at the time, I felt I was constantly out of place.
At the age of ten, we moved to another country. I was signed
up in a school where I knew no one, and couldn't speak the
language. Nothing quite like being thrown in at the deep
end! I made some friends and did my best to fit in, but no
friendship seemed to last; to my friends, I was the foreigner.

I grew up in a place where everyone knew everyone, all the
families were connected somehow, cousins were best friends
with each other, and it felt like there was little place for me. I
even became an outsider to part of my family, and I
remember some family members using that against me
during the occasional arguments, telling me that since I was
a foreigner, I had no say. Bottom line is, that I was experiencing the complete opposite of what my friends had. The
contrast was impactful.

I did make friends, but the friendships felt superficial and
short-lasting, while I was longing for meaningful friendships.
I wanted someone I could truly connect with, a best friend
of my own, but this was difficult. I felt like I had very little in
common with anyone.

Looking back, I think subconsciously I was looking for my
place and was so eager to find it, that I developed a people-

pleaser attitude. I wanted to be accepted, to feel I was part of something. But I only set myself up for disappointment; friendships that didn't work, and people taking advantage of my kindness and tolerance. I would then explode and cause arguments, or just put an end to it and break those friendships. Whether in friendship or romantic relationships, I was setting myself up for failure with that people-pleasing attitude, not to mention the expectations I had of others which would, of course, end up in disappointment.

I was expecting the same "people pleasing" attitude from my friends, which then led me to some very disappointing and painful situations in my relationships. I would get into relationships that were not right for me, and they would all go one way… I felt little and voiceless.

I've always felt something was at odds, but my discomfort really became obvious in my 20s when my romantic relationship came to an end. The feeling of being in the wrong place was very strong. I had a hunger for adventure and new experiences which were really driven by a need to belong, a hunger which I had suppressed during the five years the relationship lasted. I started working to travel, and I would spend three months abroad at a time. What I couldn't see though is that I was running away. I thought I'd find something better somewhere else.

I would look at friends' and acquaintances' lives, wondering why I couldn't have what they had because you know, the grass always looks greener on the other side… Bottom line, wanting to be accepted and to belong had turned into a very unhelpful way to address life. I was focusing on what I didn't have and felt miserable seeking something I didn't believe was available to me.

A friend and I were at my place one afternoon, talking about life and how we were feeling in general. Although for different reasons, both of us seemed to be at similar points in our lives, curious about what other places in the world might have to offer and what places were appealing to us. So, we started considering options, and this was when I finally decided to go on an adventure. It was one of the best decisions I have ever made! I moved to London.

The beginning wasn't easy but it felt right; most people are outsiders in London, which is a point you can have in common with anyone. I was no longer standing out but more like blending in. I made new friends, had new job opportunities, new experiences, and new learnings about cultures and traditions, yet something was still not right and I still felt out of place,

But how? Why couldn't I just settle?

The overall feeling I lugged around with me was "I have screwed up my life", "I wish I could start over", "I've missed the opportunities", "It's too late", and "I'll always be alone", "I'll never be happy".

I was living in the past with regrets, and focusing on the goals I hadn't reached. I couldn't understand what was happening. I believed, on a conscious level, that I deserved to be happy but I was constantly focusing on why I didn't have what I wanted. It felt like life was playing a game with me by giving me a taster of what things could look and feel like, but then it would take it away from me. I was mad at life and the universe for not giving me what I wanted. I felt hopeless.

I have now learnt that's not how it works. The universe is not trying to make me suffer, it wants to help me get what I want, but I need to help myself too by working on myself, getting clarity on what I truly want, and focusing on it. Instead, I was blocking my own manifestations and couldn't see the wood for the trees. This is actually now what I help my clients with, getting to know themselves better, and getting clarity on what they truly want to focus on.

I decided to seek support and started seeing a psychologist, who truly helped me to start looking at things differently and see that things could indeed change. I was just starting to get somewhere when the sessions stopped abruptly. At least I was in a more curious position and with a spur of hope that things could improve. I had learnt that there was plenty of time for me to turn things around.

I wasn't sure about how I would do this yet, but I suddenly had a strong feeling of "just trust the process more". It was then when the universe came into play and I felt I received three messages over a couple of days through conversations and adverts. The signs were too strong to ignore this time.

I found myself signing up for a course, and training as a life coach. This changed my life! It gave me a community, that sense of belonging I had been longing for most of my life. I even went on and qualified with Distinction, I was ecstatic! One of my proudest achievements.

This became a turning point, a completely new career opened up for me, from coaching to mentor coach, to coaching supervisor.

Work was great, and personal development was even better. I grew within the company I was "born in", as well as creating my own practice. I moved into a flat in a fairly central part of London, made new friends in the area, became more social, went back to tennis lessons, enjoyed weekends away with friends, planned a long overdue trip to Australia and finally got the dog I had wanted for years!

I was at the best point of my life. I was living the dream! But the universe seemed to have other plans...

From one day to another, my job position unexpectedly ceased to exist, and this for me, was the real turning point. I felt I had been working and fighting during the years to reach a lifestyle that I loved and had longed for, only for it to be taken away from me unexpectedly a few months later. It wasn't so much about losing the job and the salary, it was the feelings of disappointment, the loss of a community and the loneliness coming back. The discomfort and regrets seemed to be rising again.

I felt hopeless, I did not want to make any effort anymore. I had no motivation. I felt lost, with a complete lack of direction, and despair. It was time to take stock!

I gave in my notice for the flat, put it all in storage and decided to go and take a break from London, and from life in general. The main problem was travelling with the dog, him not being allowed in planes or trains made it challenging, but thankfully, a very good friend came forward and offered to drive us across the channel, so the adventure began. I decided to take three months off my life and its obligations.

Over that period, I went back to all the main cities of my childhood, reconnected with the past, and caught up with old friends, acquaintances and family. I indulged myself in savouring all my favourite dishes and pastries. The trip to Australia I had planned back in February was already booked and paid for, so two months later, it was finally time to take off for Australia with a friend and make my childhood dream come true.

I remember when I was five years old, my parents used to buy me those children's weekly magazines which came with the cassette that would read the story written in the magazine. There was one about Santa spending Christmas surfing in Australia and another about a kangaroo that got lost due to a fire and how he was struggling to find water. Thankfully the story ended well as the fire was put out and the kangaroo was reunited with his mother by a lake. That story really stuck with me, and ever since then, I had wanted to go to Australia. Now, over 30 years later, I was finally making that dream come true!

Off I went with a very good friend of mine. It was a whole month of discoveries, new experiences, and dreams that came true. I saw kangaroos in the wild, held a koala named after my favourite James Bond, Connery, and finally walked down the Bee Gees Way and through the town the brothers grew up in (forever grateful to my friend for this). I visited Uluru's rock, with the hottest temperature ever! Sadly, it was a time of massive bushfires, which I saw from the plane. But ironically, I could see how it was just like Santa in my child-hood magazine story. I also surfed at Christmas. It was an unforgettable trip, a once-in-a-lifetime event and very energising.

It was now time to come back to reality and back to Europe. I decided to spend some time in Spain, which was where I grew up. Spending time there felt good; it was full of familiar places and faces. I reconnected with friends I hadn't had the chance to see much whilst living away. After a few weeks, I started looking at flights to come back to London but before I knew it, seemingly out of the blue, the Covid-19 pandemic was upon us. Borders were closed, travel restrictions were in place, countries were locked down and we were ordered to stay at home. I felt called to stay put in Spain.

During those months, my friends and I came together. We had regular weekly calls, we signed up for courses together, we played cards together, even a special Marvel edition. I signed up for a couple of courses, I created a new programme for my clients, and I developed my cooking skills, the downside of which also meant developing my weight.

Yet I couldn't help but feel again that something was missing, the discomfort of not knowing what to do and where to settle was back and more uncomfortable than ever.

I spent months working on that internal fight with my coach, as part of me wanted to go back to London. I would get frustrated and angry as life seemed to put things into place so I couldn't or wouldn't go back... An old flame even came back into the picture. In complete honesty, I knew deep down he and I had no chance, but due to that uncomfortable feeling of not belonging again, I was forcing myself to see non-existent evidence this would work.

I was pushing so things would happen, I was allowing things that were not acceptable. I was back to an old pattern. I was lost, without knowing where I belonged.

As the discomfort and 'not belonging' feelings surfaced again, I decided to face reality and did some further internal work. I stopped trying to make choices and force things to happen. Enough was enough. This time, I was fully letting go and trusting the universe. I accepted what was. With the help of my coach, I began making peace with where I was in life, who I was, and the things that had happened to me. Or should I say, for me. And that's when things really shifted. The real trigger was surrendering. There was a first attempt at this when I moved to London and started feeling I had found my place as most people were foreigners, but this was still coming from external factors. It didn't last.

It felt life was simply wanting to see whether I had learnt my lesson the first time, which clearly, I hadn't. And only when I accepted what was, surrendered fully to what wasn't, and finally trusted the universe by letting go of expectations of what, where, and when I considered things needed to happen, the situation shifted.

I moved into a flat I love and feel so grateful for in Spain. I got my things sent to me from the UK (nothing better than having your own stuff with you!), work picked up like never before, opportunities such as being part of this book project knocked at my door, and all by surrendering to the process.

I stopped trying to figure it out and stopped pushing myself to choose a path. I let go of the reins and control. I stopped fighting what wasn't. I stopped projecting myself too much into the future and I started from the beginning.

And this is when things started to fall into place. It all started with a change of environment when I moved into this new flat. Overnight, I began feeling better. I had the new, exciting project of turning it into a home (that word rings a bell). I started a new business from scratch; I got a new logo and website, I created a vision board, and I focused on the things

I wanted to. But most importantly, I focused on who I wanted to be, and how I wanted to feel.

And this is what changed my life. I am home within myself and happy being me.

I now see how the rug being swept from underneath me in London was actually for my greatest good. It helped me grow and brought awareness to what could be changed and how. I just was trying so hard to blend in, when really, I needed to GO WITHIN.

This period wasn't the easiest but it gifted me with so much; the time to enjoy the trip of a lifetime, connect with myself, and most importantly, it freed me at a time that allowed me to care for my beloved granny in her last month of life, which I am so grateful for - a unique and fulfilling experience.

I have learnt so much about myself in this period: I have a lot of courage, I no longer run away, chasing the unknown, and I am happy where I am. I am happy with who I am. I finally embraced the fact that home is inside. You chose where you want to belong. Your best friend does not need to be someone you have known since birth; it can be you. I am now closer than ever to making my dream come true of splitting my time between the UK and Spain!

I've learned to appreciate what I have instead of what I don't, and to look for happiness inside myself and not from the outside. This is precisely what I am now supporting my clients to do, supporting them to recognise we don't "need" anyone but ourselves, looking at different perspectives and recognising that most thoughts are limiting beliefs. That assumptions, anticipation and expectations are what can cause us to feel unhappy. Once we learn to manage this, then things start shifting. It all starts from the inside, from understanding who we are and what it is we truly want.

There are so many lessons I have learnt in the past few years. Learning to put boundaries in place to stick to what feels right and aligned with my values is a big one. Many people actually struggle to say no to others, and yet, this is so important. We must learn to put ourselves first and understand that. Look inside out not outside in.

Some people are meant to be around for the whole journey and others only for parts of it. The one that counts is you; you will always be on this journey with yourself.

I see this on a daily basis; I have a variety of people I work with every day, and together we explore the situations, the challenges, and the reality they find themselves in. We look at their visions for the future, and what I find most commonly is that they are looking outside of themselves for the answers they seek.

It is only when we address what might need to change from within that the magic happens. Only once we understand what goes on inside, can we change the outside by adapting our responses. Whether we are scared of a negative response, trying to fix a toxic relationship or, like myself, chasing the

LAURE POLIDORI

unknown, as long as we keep looking outside of ourselves for answers, we will keep hitting a wall until we accept that change must first come from within.

In the past few months, I have put an end to a relationship that required too much effort to keep alive. I have let go of a toxic friendship in which I was constantly second-guessing myself and feeling guilty about not doing enough. I have let go of the anger and frustration of not being where I thought I was supposed to be. I feel content. I have new projects to look forward to, and new hopes. I like where and how I am, and this, to me, is the feeling of belonging.

Looking back to the beginning of this chapter, I can now say I have a healthier relationship with my family, I know who my true friends are, I enjoy experiences I truly care about, I have better quality relationships, I enjoy courses I truly am interested in, I have the car I've liked since I was 18, and I have a dog who is always happy to see me.

The universe sends me messages that I am still learning to decipher, and of course, I continue to face challenges, but I have learnt to surrender to, as opposed to fighting those signs, and now I don't think that life is going against me by not giving me what I want.

I now work in harmony with the universe. I see that when things go off track, it's going to somehow be for my greater good. I have to trust, show up as my best self, and grow through my life experiences. After all, we're here for a good time, not a long time.

MY FIVE KEY TAKEAWAYS

1. Decide to start your day in a positive way, however that looks for you. Making sure you step with your 'right foot' first, helps start your day as you mean to go on.
2. Choose a daily motivational quote. Whether it's through a page-a-day calendar of inspirational quotes, an app, affirmation cards, or writing your own down, choosing a quote to take with you through the day helps you stay in alignment.
3. Prioritise moving your body and getting fresh air. I love taking my dog for a walk first thing, with my soya latte in hand, and with a no phone policy! This helps ground you and gives you head space, ready to make the most of the day.
4. Review your schedule for the day. Not only does this prepare the mind for what's to come, but it supports you in keeping a good balance of work and play. If there's all work and no play, something has to change!
5. Give yourself permission to wind down at the end of the day. I like to make sure I have an hour's wind down by either watching an episode of one of my favourite TV shows or reading a chapter of a non-work-related book. Journaling is also a firm favourite to reflect back on the day, and state what I'm grateful for in life.

I trust that each reader will find their own takeaway from my chapter.

ABOUT THE AUTHOR

LAURE POLIDORI

Laure (pronounced Lor) is a Coach Mentor who, using her transformational somatic approach to coaching, focuses on the deep connection between mind and body, and how each is intricately interlinked with one another. Laure's passion for mentoring, coaching, and coach supervision is driven by the extraordinary results self-reflection has had for her many clients.

Laure previously worked in international trade, and as a French and Spanish tutor, joining the coaching community well over a decade ago. Laure's unique gift is being able to speak fluent English, French, and Spanish, which allows her to work with a great variety of people from all over the world.

As an avid lover of excitement and fun, Laure is a self-confessed adrenaline junkie. She never hesitates in seeking out new experiences like skydiving or bungee jumping and rides all kinds of rollercoasters. On Laure's days off, you'll most likely find her skiing, either on snow or water. At home, Laure's newfound interest in pyrography is helping her reconnect with her creative side.

Laure is available for transformational somatic one-on-one sessions, and group coach mentoring, coaching, and coach supervision sessions.

You can reach Laure at:

Email : laure.polidori@gmail.com

Website: www.poli-coaching.com

facebook.com/LPCoachingSupervision

instagram.com/poli_coaching

linkedin.com/in/laurepolidori

8

ALIGNING TO A LIFE THAT LIGHTS YOU UP!

SAMANTHA LYNCH

I'm sitting in my garden as I've just finished work. The sun is shining, my dog is sunbathing, and my other half is sitting beside me, reading his book. It's 6.30 pm on a Thursday and I'm looking forward to no work at the weekend and catching up with friends. There's a fridge full of food and a few quid still left in the bank, despite it being three days until the end of the month and payday!

It wasn't always this way though.

I don't spend hours commuting back and forth to work anymore.

Looking back to my early career, I'd be waiting for the number 32 bus to take me up the East Lancs to the Manchester Arndale on a Saturday morning. There were often mornings when it didn't arrive; usually, this was when it was raining. It was like GM Buses had a sixth sense and knew when to make you have not just a bad day, but a really bad day. Arriving to work late and drenched, with expectations of you being the epitome of "The face of Manchester's finest retail outlet", while delivering an amazing customer experience - and all this first thing in the morning, before coffee!

Fast forward to a few years BC (before Covid), I'd often be sat in traffic at the Jack Lynch tunnel in Cork, waiting for a gap in said traffic to head on the link to the office. You'd be waiting a while... especially if a lorry had attempted to travel through said tunnel but was too tall to get through. Despite the multiple signs and sensors, this could happen two to three times a week, and when it did, you were going nowhere for a while. Getting to and from work was tricky and tedious.

These days, I get to walk my dog at lunchtime, I'm able to put a wash on in the afternoon and prepare our evening meal in advance, which in turn allows me to head out for a swim after a busy work day. It's the small things. I feel less stressed and more productive. Something I once only dreamed of.

As I said earlier, it wasn't always this way. That is why I will never take these things for granted.

I'm Sam. I work for a global tech company and I look after learning and enablement for worldwide sales and customer success teams. What does that mean in non-corporate speak? I help sales and customer-focused teams (and their managers) to do more and be more effective by using training and coaching to develop their knowledge and skills. These are the fantastic people that work to secure and take care of our customers; carrying targets and service levels on their shoulders, which are delivered through a wealth of knowledge and an aptitude for building great relationships.

It's a Monday to Friday job. Hours are varied and can sometimes mean an early start to talk with colleagues in Australia or Singapore. Training teams in San Francisco can often mean later calls in the evening.

BC, this often meant travelling to different locations across the globe to deliver workshops and facilitate team training and coaching. Considering I never set foot on a plane until I was 21, I'm forever grateful for the opportunity to travel - even if, on occasion, it is more of a flying visit. More often than not, the itinerary can look like this:

Airport - Plane - Office - Hotel - Office - Plane - Airport - Home.

If you've travelled for work, you'll know it is not as glamorous as Instagram makes out, but travelling and working with different cultures lights me up and is an opportunity that I always thrive upon.

Working remotely for the last six years had given me the flexibility to try to have a more manageable work day - *try* being the operative word. If you work remotely or have switched to home working in the last few years, you'll know what I mean.

For years, I struggled with the concept of "work-life balance" and the **_worrier_** in me often made sure the balance tipped firmly on the work side of the scales.

These days, the **_Warrior_** in me focuses more on work-life harmony, enabling me to make better decisions with my time based on my priorities and as a result, I have become more productive. One of the benefits of this is that I'm able to participate in amazing projects such as this one or take part in mentoring women in business or those just starting in their careers. The challenge of being a woman in tech - which can show up as very much a "man's world" - is real. While companies are much more aware of diversity, equity and inclusion in 2022, there is still some work to do.

So how did I become less of a worrier and more of a Warrior, who stepped into a version of me that, in my 40s, I now feel more comfortable and confident with? When was the awakening that made me listen to the real voice inside that mattered?

I'd say it was after I hit the bottom. When I didn't have the energy to get out of bed. I had no appetite and, as such, couldn't eat more than a slice of toast or a tiny salad. I wasn't sleeping well at night, as the tiresome chatter in my mind would keep me awake, reminding me how much of a failure I was and how I was completely sucking at life.

Now here's the thing. I'm not advocating you get into a place of deep darkness.

In fact, I highly discourage it. If you're struggling, the last thing you are sometimes physically able to do is to make that initial step to "get help".

During this point of despair, my thought process was that I must go through some "tough life lessons" to get to a slightly better place and that much of what happened to me was deserved, and often my doing.

"Well, it is what it is" mixed with "#positivevibesonly" was my way of coping.

"These things always happen to me," and "What else would you expect?" were part of my daily thought pattern, and I would be the first to say this to my friends when we got together. I couldn't see how the perception I had about myself and my life was impacting my day-to-day life.

Thinking of being more spiritual and more in tune with my authentic self mustered up visions of yoga, meditation and being thought of as hippy-dippy among my corporate colleagues. My perception, in this instance, was very much my reality, and I was afraid to step into my own power for fear of how I would be judged. At that moment, the worst judgement I was feeling was coming from within me, and it was soul-destroying.

However, through a series of defining moments, which I'll call "**_Lightbulb Moments_**", I took decisive steps to help me move forward and become my authentic self. I now find my resilience is high, my blood pressure is low, and I'm able to rise up in times of challenge, adversity, and success.

Prior to this transformation, I would come across as positive, on my game, and successful, yet inside, I would be riddled with self-doubt for starters, a fear of failure as the main course, and a massive bowl of imposter syndrome for dessert.

Knowing what I know now about our mind-body connection, it's no wonder I was walking around with permanent heartburn and indigestion!

So, without further ado, allow me to share the lightbulb moments that mattered, and how they transformed my life.

LIGHTBULB MOMENT 1:

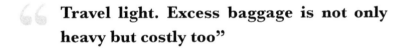 **Travel light. Excess baggage is not only heavy but costly too"**

You'll probably sense a pattern here that I like to travel, so what better defining moment to start us off than one that relates to travel? Kind of…

For years, I felt like I was carrying a huge suitcase full of rocks around with me. Not one of these modern suitcases with wheels and a handy pull-out handle. Oh no. Old school, brown leather, massive, family-size suitcase. Full of rocks.

Each rock was grey and heavy. It weighed a ton - on my mind and on my heart. These rocks had been 'gifted' to me by people and events from my past - how very kind of them.

- The girl that bullied me in secondary school, for no other reason than I was in the top set for Maths and she wasn't.
- The lads that laughed at me because I didn't have the most expensive trainers when I was on the netball team.
- The ex-partner that ridiculed me for more reasons than I have space to write here.
- The friend that was self-serving and was great at offloading onto me, but not great at lending an ear when I needed one.
- The customer that waited for me outside work, to verbally and physically abuse me because I wouldn't replace their water-damaged mobile phone.
- The senior leader at work had a serious issue with me being a woman and having an opinion on a topic that was an area of my expertise. Who banged his fist on the table in a complete rage, and ridiculed my work efforts in front of my boss and other colleagues.
- The C-level executive who told me that "You will definitely feel imposter syndrome working here" which went on to completely amplify the imposter syndrome I was already feeling.

In many instances, these 'gifts' were from people who were supposed to be my allies and my champions – instead, they passed judgement and criticised me for wanting to be better, and do better.

The expectations and opinions of others lay heavy on my mind and anchored themselves to my heart. Every time it happened I felt the same. Hurt and upset. Sometimes angry; mostly frustrated.

WHY ME?

Every time something happened, another rock went into the suitcase. Grey and heavy.

The impact of this weight was often huge - a deadly cocktail of jetlag mixed with anxiety caused a lack of sleep.

Doubt and lack of self-worth caused me to over-plan and over-prepare for every eventuality, in turn, adding to my stress levels.

My thoughts definitely started to become things, making it OK for me to feel like I deserved the way I was feeling. It was like I had made peace with being in conflict with myself.

I almost expected the worst to happen, waiting for the inevitable.

Yet on the outside, I looked fine. I felt fine. This was always my go-to line if anyone asked.

Living in Ireland for a while meant I had added the phrase "oh, you know yourself... I'm grand!" to my vocabulary when anyone asked how I was doing.

My happy disposition and sunshine-yellow personality traits shone through and helped me get by the day-to-day hustle.

By the time my marriage broke down, the only thing that was fine was the collection of rocks in the old suitcase. It was a fine collection indeed.

Inside, I was far from fine. It was at this point I knew something had to change.

Knowing there had to be a better way, I set about working on myself - a journey of self-discovery and self-care. I started with counselling, then onto swimming, and then a better diet.

Taking one day at a time and initially, on a very tactical level, I began to feel stronger and more resilient.

Drawing strength from the small wins spurred me on to head back to college to further develop my skill set. Taking some practical action at home, my next step was to sort my finances out. Being on my own meant making some tough choices at the time, but my priority was that my mortgage was paid and my bills were settled every month.

The hard work at college paid off and this enabled me to go for a promotion at work and command a slightly higher salary, which provided a little more in the way of financial freedom - not completely worry-free, but in a position that I knew I could manage my overheads and at the same time start to put a little away each month. That feeling of not living every month to the absolute wire, despite working your butt off, brought a small sense of relief.

Piece by piece, my feelings started to change. The weight on my shoulders started to shift, yet somehow, I was still holding myself back. When it came to changing careers and the opportunity to travel to different countries came with it, my excitement was dampened by the weight of the luggage that came with me. This is from a person that actually does travel light. I refined my approach to packing my bag and refined my approach to carrying around other people's expectations in my suitcase. Both were extremely beneficial, given the circumstances.

I found that "Misery loves Company" and that there was an element of toxicity within my peer group. My growth meant that my friendship circle evolved, and my relationship status changed - both for the better. My vibe most definitely started to attract my tribe.

This was just the beginning. Knowing there was more work to do, I sought out a coach who was on my wavelength but who had the ability to push me out of my comfort zone. This is where I had my second lightbulb moment.

LIGHTBULB MOMENT 2:

 Whether you think you can or whether you think you can't, you're right"

— HENRY FORD

Working with my coach on practising gratitude and using Timeline Therapy and CBT, we started to undo some of the biases that I'd brought with me over the years. We went backwards to go forwards on a journey of discovery and enlightenment.

The rocks I'd been gifted needed to go, and by golly, did we leave them behind.

How did I change that mindset?

- Undoing the stories that I'd taught myself to be true.
- Journaling more and being grateful for what I had, instead of longing for what I didn't.
- Going back to that child-like state, where dreams are big and anything is possible because you say it is so!

I mean, when do we decide you have to "become an adult" and at what point do we bring the dreaming to a halt as the limiting beliefs take over?

For me, it was many years ago and I had enough of it holding me back. There was only one way forward - to face my fears head-on, and focus on where those limiting beliefs had come from.

WHY WAS THIS IMPORTANT?

Well, it didn't matter how much feedback I got that said things were great or how much impact I could see from my work and deliverables - I genuinely thought I wasn't good enough and I *needed* to do more… to *be* better. My thought patterns and inner critic told me I wasn't good enough and therefore, I was right! This is exactly how it played out.

I kept saying yes to people and taking on more work, which involved trying to validate my feelings through my output. This meant overworking on most days and feeling under-valued while doing it. A double-edged sword and a recipe for disaster.

I NEEDED TO GET OUT OF MY OWN WAY.

Having let go of the crippling limiting beliefs means I now think "I CAN", and therefore, I DO!

How has this benefited me? As recently as six months ago, I went through a gruelling interview phase to secure a senior role that, in the past, I had told myself my gender, location, and ability would not be enough to secure. And yet, here I am, doing it from my home office in Ireland, and loving the company and people I work with. I have peace of mind, knowing there is salary parity in line with my counterparts of the opposite sex, who also work in the same industry and within a similar role.

Knowing my worth and awakening my authentic, confident self paid dividends when it came to negotiating the new package - something I would advise others to do in the past, but never quite cracked it myself. What was most refreshing is that my employer at the time of onboarding did not hesitate, as they worked from a place of total reward, which was based on your experience, skill set and industry knowledge. All those years, I knew deep down I deserved better, yet was happy to settle for less. The moment I worked on my self-worth and accepted myself as the Warrior Woman I truly am, my outcomes changed ten-fold. It was like an invisible signal was sent out that said "SAM IS READY FOR MORE!".

LIGHTBULB MOMENT 3:

 What other people think of me is none of my business"

It took me a long time to come to peace with this mantra. After all, I was an avid collector of rocks, which often translated into other people's opinions.

There will always be a cohort of people that are more concerned with who does what, both in and outside of work, and in a corporate setting, there are many opportunities for this kind of poison to spread. I'm not one for being judgey or gossipy. I've always struggled to understand what kick people get out of this kind of behaviour.

A great woman named Eleanor Roosevelt once said:

 Great minds discuss ideas; average minds discuss events; small minds discuss people."

I guess that sheds a little light on the rationale of why they do it.

SO HOW DID I MAKE PEACE WITH THIS, AFTER ALL THOSE YEARS?

Considering I always cared what people thought of me, and bearing in mind this thought process went as far back as school, putting this one to sleep was going to be tricky.

Or was it?

You've just heard me say that *"Whether I think I can or whether I think I can't, I'm probably right"* was my Lightbulb Moment number 2, and I had to channel this to have my third lightbulb shine clearly and brightly. The moment my thought process went from giving a damn about their chatter to giving more of a damn about *my* headspace, and how I spoke to myself. This is when my perspective changed.

Being more mindful and checking in with myself helped regulate my inner peace, and as the days went by and this habit became the norm, so did my feelings towards what others may or may not think of me.

The reason for this? I now value how I think of myself more and need zero validation from others as a result. I talk to myself as if I was talking to my best friend, with kindness, humility, empathy and respect. Examples of this include:

- What would I say to her to make her feel validated?
- How would I encourage her to help her feel more positive?
- How would I let her know that it is ok not to feel ok?
- What could I ask her to make her think differently?
- What type of assistance could I offer to help her regain her confidence?

I no longer berate myself because of other people's perceptions and, as part of the process, ensure I do not take myself too seriously. Regaining my love for what I do and how I live my life, alongside spending more time with the important people in it, has provided me with further balance and perspective. Should I find myself listening to the non-important voices and perspectives that occasionally hum away in the background, my 'best friend' chimes in with a healthy dose of "cop on" and reminds me to focus on thoughts and things that serve me better.

What this has also meant is that I am more open to receiving considered feedback that often has the best intentions. As a result, I am more likely to act upon it. Having the ability to discern between acting upon ill-informed opinions, and reflecting on well-informed feedback has been hugely beneficial to my development in the last five years.

LIGHTBULB MOMENT 4:

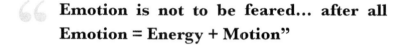 **Emotion is not to be feared... after all Emotion = Energy + Motion"**

In business, there is often a train of thought that says you should leave emotion at the door.

As a woman in business, often you are deemed 'too emotional" if you show any ounce of reaction or sentiment towards something that upsets you, you feel passionate about, or that you don't agree with.

People far wiser than me, have often said that the word "Emotion" translates to "Energy in Motion".

The moment I took time to internalise this, things became clearer.

HOW DID I SEE THIS DIFFERENTLY?

I'll start by saying I would sometimes get upset about things that frustrated me at work because I gave a damn. I would often become animated about things that excited me because I gave a damn.

As a caring empath who has high extroverted energy, this would typically show up in my action-orientated ways, with a massive dollop of fairness, consideration, and helpfulness to boot. I mean, come on - I have the word "Enablement" in my job title!

I enjoy enabling things to work, enabling people to help them be more effective, and generally getting stuff done. Yet for many years, I felt like I could not be myself or express myself freely in fear of judgement, which massively impacted my mental and spiritual wellbeing.

Once I had lightbulb moment number 3 cracked, I worried less about what people thought of me (and applied the "nun-ya" principle, as my other half would say - "none-of-your-business!").

This gave me more confidence to get to grips with the emotion piece. Showing up as my authentic self meant that I appeared (and continue to do so) in a way that demonstrates that I care and I basically give a damn. I'm aligned with my values instead of being in conflict with them.

It is far better to lead with authenticity and an element of vulnerability than to come across as someone who is perceived as inauthentic and as such, finds themselves wearing a mask that they are unable to keep straight all the time. By bringing the best version of myself to work, I feel more energised - when you're keeping up a pretence, it's flipping exhausting.

LIGHTBULB MOMENT 5:

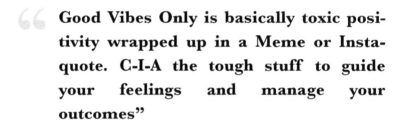 **Good Vibes Only is basically toxic positivity wrapped up in a Meme or Instaquote. C-I-A the tough stuff to guide your feelings and manage your outcomes"**

If you're on any form of social media, over the last few years you may have seen plenty of posts talking about "Good Vibes Only" or "#PositiveVibes".

I'm all about positivity and having a positive attitude. I'm a glass-half-full kinda lass.

But what about the days you're just not feeling it? You're having a day that is the exact opposite of positive? The days when you are genuinely feeling a little weary or overwhelmed.

Resilience is key. My focus here is really straightforward; instead of me saying "why is this happening to me?", I flip that and ask "what am I learning from this?" or "what is this teaching me?"

HOW DO I CONTINUE TO BRING MY BEST SELF TO THE FOREFRONT?

First of all, I'm proud to say I'm a Warrior Woman. Less of a worrier, and definitely more focused on visualising what I want to achieve and how I want to feel when I've done it.

It started by reclaiming my commute to focus on myself every morning and going from there. So, the time I used to spend waiting for the bus or sitting in traffic, I now spend investing in my mindset, and mental wellbeing and figuring out how to best spend my workday.

If you're wondering what this consists of, I'll share some of my top tips - both spiritual and practical - to keep my inner Warrior fully charged!

Occasionally, I'll do a short meditation

I still struggle to hush the chatterbox in my head when it comes to meditation! If you think of a web browser with 26 tabs open, that is often my brain. However, the benefits when I take time to focus and meditate are noticeable on my mood, my productivity and my general approach to the day. Check out YouTube or the Calm app for shorter meditation and mindfulness options if, like me, meditation doesn't come naturally to you.

Connecting with being mindful through holding or carrying a crystal

When I first started working with my coach, she sent me a gift of 3 crystals. One of which was Amethyst - my Nanna's birthstone. Not only do I feel energy through crystals in general, this one, in particular, makes me feel that much closer to her. She was a proper powerhouse of a lady, an original Warrior, so it's no wonder my vibrations are high when I'm connected with that particular crystal!

A quick "check-in" with myself to see how I am feeling on a scale of 1-10

- I do this by putting my hand on my heart and asking myself the question "How am I feeling today on a scale of 1-10?"
- Taking this approach allows me to determine how I am feeling in the moment: if a high score, how can I stay in high vibration? If I get a low score, what one thing can I do to take me up one point on the scale? I instantly start to feel more on top of things, regardless of my number. By doing this small daily practice, I've stopped masking feelings and continued to make progress - even on tricky days. My "what one thing?" is also an approach in other areas of my life and in my coaching practice.

Focusing on my prioritised tasks - taking a practical "what's my first thing first?" approach

- To do this effectively, I make a conscious effort to swerve my email first thing as this is often everyone else's to-do list! Another tip here is that "instant message doesn't mean instant reply" so, if you are getting productive, try muting your IMs and notifications for a while. They will still be there in 20 minutes when you have completed your 'first thing first'.

Manifesting what I want to achieve

- This involves thinking about what I want to happen instead of what I don't want to happen
- Trusting the process to demonstrate that I am open to new things and by doing so, welcome in the possibility of new opportunities and feelings
- As a result, my vibration is high and more often than not, good things that I desire come my way.
- It's amazing where you find opportunities if you are open to it. If your mindset is what's known as 'closed' or 'fixed', you cannot expect anything to change in the way you desire, as you simply won't be able to see the wood for the trees. Keeping your mind and heart open to all possibilities means nothing is out of reach.

Time blocking my day to be more productive

- This mostly works out for me, although there are days when utter chaos breaks loose! That's work for you. By ensuring that I have not only required tasks, but time for things that light me up and that align with my values and goals somewhere in the week means I often have things to look forward to.
- These spur me on through the conflicting priorities, short deadlines, and general tough times that arise.
- Visualising how I want to feel at the end of a task keeps me focused. It gets my head out of the task and into the sense of achievement that comes with the end result.

Eating better and hydrating well

- Taking time to enjoy lunch is the first step! Getting away from my desk, being mindful for a few minutes and then enjoying my lunch. Plus water - lots of it. A far cry from grabbing a pasty from Greggs in the Arndale Centre and running back into work.
- If you know me, and you've read this far, you will be thinking this isn't the Sam we know. To celebrate, bubbles are often on the menu! Matching a tipple with a glass of water definitely aids my recovery and minimises the self-sabotage hangover fear the next day.

What about when things get out of control? I'm a realist, I know this happens.

While at college, a Coaching Lecturer taught us the CIA technique.

Control - Influence - Accept.

- What do I have some control over?
- What can I do or where can I influence the outcome?
- What do I have to just accept and suck it up?

A definite leveller and if you're not feeling overly spiritual, CIA is a focused and practical tool to help you feel more on top of things.

Often, the influence question is reminding myself that I can influence the outcome of something if I look at it differently, or I remind myself how I want to feel when it is done.

I invite you to check in with yourself and determine whether you resonate with the lightbulb moments I've shared. Should you find yourself in a pattern where you are struggling with overwhelm or self-doubt, pick one or two of the Warrior top tips and practice them for at least two weeks to really reap the benefit. Habit forming takes time, and is truly life-changing. Now go light up your life!

MY FIVE KEY TAKEAWAYS (AKA MY LIGHTBULB MOMENTS)

1. Travel light. Excess baggage is not only heavy but costly too.
2. Whether you think you can or whether you think you can't, you're right.
3. What other people think of me is none of my business.
4. Emotion is not to be feared… after all, Emotion = Energy + Motion.
5. "Good Vibes Only" is basically toxic positivity wrapped up in a Meme or Insta-quote. C-I-A the tough stuff to guide your feelings and manage your outcomes.

ABOUT THE AUTHOR

SAMANTHA LYNCH

Samantha Lynch is responsible for global sales learning & enablement within a corporate tech company. Couple this with being a Fellow of the Learning & Performance Institute and certified Leadership & Life Coach, Sam leads with her head, and her heart. As a strong facilitator, curious discoverer, and a patient listener, Sam partners with teams and individuals to unlock their potential through actionable learning and removing limiting beliefs by challenging personal blockers.

Having invested in her professional development for over 13 years, Sam decided to embark on a journey of self-discovery three years ago and her inner warrior was awakened, enlightening her with a deep sense of "more warrior, less worrier!"

In her spare time, Sam is a volunteer mentor to women looking to either kickstart their career or springboard their own business. She uses her skills as a mental health first aider to be a light in times of darkness.

Sam is the missus to Mr Lynch and doggy mum to Deefor - a lockdown foster pup who never went back to the rescue! She is a Scouser who lives in Ireland as an adopted Corkonian - blending Liverpudlian wit with Irish humour in her day-to-day. With a passion for travel, gigs and food, she's often found trying to combine all of these and loves to fill her cup (or glass!) full of the good stuff.

Sam is available for 1:1 Sales, Leadership & Life coaching (in person or virtually), event panels & speaker opportunities, and mentoring.

You can connect with Sam on:

 twitter.com/learninglynch

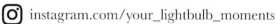 instagram.com/your_lightbulb_moments

 linkedin.com/in/samanthalancashirelynch

9

AWAKENING THROUGH 'IN-LIGHTENMENT'

SARAH RODGER JONES

As I begin to write this chapter, I am sitting in the beautiful closet-come-office space I recently created. My desk, as well as the rest of the house, is adorned with happy pictures and meaningful belongings that evoke joy, gratitude, and inspiration. Light floods in from an east-facing window that looks out to the garden which I have happily tended for the past seven years, a place of meditation and fulfilment. The sound of birdsong and the *clippity-clop* of a passing horse and rider carries on the gentle summer breeze. My home, surrounded by the Welsh countryside, is my place of peace. The feelings and sensations I now enjoy I have been seeking all of my adult life. I am living the reality of a dream I once thought was unattainable. "How?" you may ask. Through so much hard soul work and, like my home and garden, continuous imperfect progress.

I derive so much happiness from my personal life. I am surrounded by great souls, some connected by blood and others drawn by cosmic consciousness. My greatest joy is time spent with my true loves - a large family of relatives and friends, especially my precious young son. Those who know me best would describe me as a spiritualist, an academic, healer, dreamer, writer, dancer, singer, comedian, gardener, foodie, and naturalist… and I completely agree with all of those, but I am also so much more. My passions and pleasures are far-reaching.

Spiritually, I am still very much in a process of growth and self-discovery which, I believe, is how life is supposed to be; a quest for dynamic universal wisdom that is meant to be shared. I am always seeking an improved love and acquaintance with myself, who I really am, and what I really want during this life. Just when I settle into comfortable familiarity, a major *plot twist* changes the direction of my story and starts a new search, deeper again, into the centre of my soul. Soul knowledge comes to me in silent moments. I still hold a strong connection to my practice and reference to traditional religion, ancient pagan wisdom, metaphysics, and the 'light' inspiration of others. I like to call this *"in-lightened"*, for the illumination and euphoria that I feel from being in the presence of soul-minded people. My spiritual roots run very deep; however, I did not start out as such a mystic Universalist. My earliest memories take me back to the religion I was born and raised in, which shaped every core belief I once held.

When I look back at the aforementioned *plot twists* across my own timeline, three threads of metamorphosis appear that have led to my awakening: leaving a fundamentalist religion, the complex process of unlearning the conditioning I never felt aligned to, and the search for a wholly meaningful life.

These experiences led me to the continuum of shedding soul layers to develop a new relationship and knowing of myself... realising my Truth and actual identity as a sentient being. The following experiences are from a book I am currently writing and the journals I keep; the windows to my soul.

I am so proud of how far I have travelled in my spiritual and personal life, having burgeoned from a suffocating fundamentalist Christian faith, in rural America. The long and painful process of leaving my religion was about unlearning and freeing myself. Eating from *the forbidden tree* allowed me to feel all the experiences and grab so many opportunities that I otherwise would have missed. I am still deconditioning. I am the daughter inspired by my powerful feminine ancestors: every artist, nun, witch, sage, warrior, doula, soothsayer, and trailblazer.

All my life, I felt called to write. In childhood, I wanted to be both pious and rebellious. Verbally, I managed to suppress my curiosities like a good girl. I would journal my true feelings and contemplations but feared that putting pen to paper would reveal who I really was, and then I would surely be 'cast out'. I would read and reread my work, perhaps to memorise it, then shred it beyond recovery, or take it outside and ceremonially cremated the evidence.. What I would give to read the burnt manuscripts from that period of my life. Today, I feel privileged and elated to be a part of this book collaboration, a feather in my cap, and two fingers up to institutional suppression and book burners, past and present. Even as I write this, I am listening to my soul and doing heart-led work.

On one hand, the (male) leaders of our faith would preach about a woman being the 'neck that turned the head' and how valuable wives were to their husbands. The inferiority was not explicitly stated, but still celebrated; a woman's place was in the home caring for her family, being "fruitful and becoming many" as the bible commands. I silently watched the pain and suffering of my spiritual sisters. The subservience that led to sexual and financial abuse was unspoken because it would be like speaking out against God's will, heresy.

My sweet, beautiful sister was my first experience of this huge 'cover-up'. At around 14 years old, she was sexually abused by one of the elders, her teacher. I did not know what rape or molestation meant, but from my poor parents' reaction, I could tell that it was irrevocable and devastating. The church became embroiled in the investigation of my sister's allegations, the only witness to the crimes against her. They convinced my parents to drop charges as 'it was not the Christian thing to do'. My sister, violated and broken, would spend the next decade of her life in and out of mental health facilities, making multiple attempts to take her life. At the age of 23, my sister overdosed and peacefully fell asleep forever. Suffering moral trauma, our whole family permanently changed, but it drew us closer together. This was the end of my parent's involvement in the religion. They left swiftly and bravely. Suffering such a great loss and watching my parents walk that journey was profound, it lit a light in my warrior heart and later, my work for social justice.

As a female under fundamentalist religion, I struggled to fit into the skin of perfection that never felt right. By the age of 16, I was pushing the boundaries of self-expression in my dress, music, movement, questioning, and writing. In a seemingly innocuous act, I chose to have my hair cut into a chin-length bob blended into razor edging to the back of my head. That same evening, I attended church and I could instantly feel all eyes on the rear of my freshly shaven head. After the service, the elders pulled me aside to express their disappointment and distaste for my *'worldly'* hairstyle. They were the judge and jury. I was shamed and degraded in that moment, but also felt acidic anger welling from the pit of my stomach into my chest and throat. Looking back, I now understand that my choice of haircut was an unconscious response shortly after my third (and final) request for baptism was denied. I can still see that beautiful weeping girl. I can see the details of her childhood bedroom. I can see her clutching her chest whilst lying across the bed, believing she was unworthy and would never be good enough or spiritual enough for God's love. I was every woman scorned and burned for trying to live according to the forces of nature and the inexplicable spirit that churned within.

A few weeks later and I was sat down, *intervention style,* by a family I had grown very close to. They had encouraged me to leave my parent's home. It was recommended that I cut off ties with my own family once they had all left the religion, considered to be a bad influence on my spiritual growth. Although I always had a sense of love and belonging from my family, I was terrified to leave the church and face the inevitable public shame of shunning. The same familiar, acidic feeling bubbled into my throat. I did not respond but I knew it was time to leave, my chance for escape, my turning point.

Losing my religion was the easy part. Gradually, I stopped attending the five hours of weekly services, bringing a halt to my social life. My parents taught me how to leave the religion by severing all ties, like a beheading. I had left public school at 14 and chose home-schooling, having been bullied for my beliefs, so I found my family my only great source of support. My close connection to my *spiritual family* had been severed and they would pass by like complete strangers, encounters impossible to avoid in a small rural community. My new reality was both heaven and hell.

I became reacquainted with my school classmates and went a bit *wild*. It was scary and fantastic to answer every temptation: drinking, experimenting with illicit drugs and partying like a regular hedonist. Allowing myself to take lovers and 'let go', my feminine sexuality burst into bloom. A couple of years later, I was recovering from an early miscarriage, broke, uneducated, drinking and smoking heavily, with no real prospects. It seemed as though I had nothing to give, but so much to lose if I remained stuck in that place and period of my life for one more day.

The last to leave the religion and the nest, I suppose I stayed with my parents as long as I did to ensure they were going to be okay in the years following my sister's suicide. I needed their blessing to go, which they gave to me with all their hearts. I knew I was faced with another *plot twist*, so with all my courage, I packed up my belongings and headed east into the sunrise. I left on my terms but leaving my parents and everything familiar was heart-wrenching. Logistically and spiritually, I was fleeing from the memories, placed-based triggers, and fear of eventual Armageddon. What I could not escape was the belief that I was nothing more than a sinner destined for a fiery end. Unlearning this engrained falsehood would take more time. Up to that point, my move across the United States was the bravest and most independently alive I had ever felt.

Apart from becoming fiercely independent, I felt I was behind in every aspect of life outside of the protection of my parents and faith, vulnerable from inexperience. My past subservience and financial dependency had given me a mindset of inadequacy and scarcity. When entering the workforce, all of my training and promotion was centred around productivity and this is where I placed my worth. I focused on getting educated and working tirelessly in unrewarding roles to get myself 'up to speed' in the real world. Higher learning was discouraged by the church, so naturally, I took a class in college which explored different religions around the world through the medium of art, a form of once forbidden iconography. I wanted to learn everything I could about the *'wicked system of things'*, particularly other faiths and spiritual practices I was banned from exploring. I likened the decade that followed to my spiritual exodus, my time in the *wilderness*, the most disconnected I ever felt from my spiritual self. I craved a heartfelt connection that could not be fulfilled by romance or friendship. I think I was craving *me*. I did not stop searching for spiritual meaning through religion, turning to Judaism to soothe my longing. Again, I found myself leaving a religion I was never fully accepted into due to my mother not being Jewish and my disdain for any sort of male dominance.

As my university career was coming to an end, I decided to use dance and music as an outlet for stress release. In the dance department, I found new ways to use my body to convey messages. I choreographed several pieces to abstract music on controversial topics regarding social justice and my childhood trauma. The studios were a safe space to practice intense yoga and meditation. Reciting mantras and tuning out of the space and into myself enabled me to reframe every idea I had about spirituality. One morning, my instructor directed the class to visualise someone or something that had caused great pain and suffering and then to imagine absolving the source of such grief. The room was filled with voices of so many injured souls and the more the mantra cycled, the fewer voices I heard, until my voice was the only sound, repeating, "May you have peace. May you have happiness. May you be free from suffering." When we were called to finish, I had an epiphany. Tears of gratitude were streaming down my face. At that moment, I felt pure love, worth, forgiveness, and peace, for myself and others. I was finally free from the chains of anger and fear. What a feeling! On that day, I met my true self and awakened spiritually for the very first time in my life.

I made the years of my higher education count, still (unconsciously) fearful I was living on borrowed time (with Armageddon looming). I completed university in 2008, at the top of a very large graduating class. In those six years, I acquired an Associate's Degree, two Bachelor's Degrees in the Sciences, and a Minor in Dance. My education empowered me to travel abroad for my research and dissertation work. Along the way, I met my now-husband. After 'turning the tassel' four times I felt both in- and en- lightened, and engaged. I was proud to be what the elders referred to as *worldly* and well-read. I felt full of hope and ready to start my life as a real grown-up.

Until I had awakened, I placed much of my worth on the work that I was doing and projecting the outward appearance of success. Naturally, my parents were my earliest example of hard work, dedication, and love. I am so grateful to them for all of their sacrifice for my siblings and me. We were raised to be good, honest, and service-oriented success stories. Mum worked from the home as a traditional stay-at-home wife and mother, big boots to fill. My father, a workaholic, earned excellent wages and was a wonderful provider, in exchange for extremely long hours, chronic exhaustion, and a short temper, to put it mildly. My time at university was my way to honour their sacrifice, to acknowledge that I too, was not only hardworking but clever and successful... for a girl.

I am grateful that divine timing allowed me to be a part of two, unrelated, opportunities for service in historically unprecedented times:

Before college, I worked as an airline supervisor at Washington Dulles Airport. I enjoyed watching loved ones reunited and felt pangs of empathy each time I witnessed a sad goodbye. It was rewarding to send people off to make their own happy memories, or to ensure everyone and everything ran on time. I felt powerful being known as a '*ball buster*' by my colleagues, taking no bull from unruly passengers or crew. I rose to my last position quickly, taking every opportunity for training and development. During and after the September 11th attacks, I recognised that I was skilled at remaining poised under pressure and I could be of service even in catastrophic circumstances. I watched the intracompany news reels come over the printers and was haunted by the lists of all the souls lost that day. Every level of airline staffing was traumatised by those events. As an empath, I think of the weeks and months around that time, the fog of fear and grief that gripped the public and the travel industry. I wanted to be a part of the healing. I wanted to save lives and restore peace.

I attended an airport-sponsored major incident training, as well as aircraft 'ditching' in flight attendant training. The thrilling feeling of adrenaline, surging through my body as I rushed into each mock scenario, stayed with me. Inspired by Rev. Fred Rogers' quote to "look for the helpers" in times of crisis, I knew, in those moments of distress, that I could be counted on as a helper. Years later, this spurred me to go back to school and answer the work I felt called to do. I left my career in aviation, elated by my first taste of success.

I qualified as a nurse at the start of the Covid-19 pandemic. I am humbled and privileged to be a part of people's whole life journeys and honoured to work alongside other care-givers. The most rewarding moments are when I know I have saved a life. Too often, there are times when the pressure and, seemingly impossible, expectations are so heavy that I feel as though I will collapse under the weight. I struggle to balance the expectations of modern healthcare frameworks with my need to deliver the best holistic care experience for every patient. When I experience workplace conflict or moral injury, I use reflection to help me make sense. Reflection is a central part of evidence-based practice, hammered into every nursing student's head, and certainly into mine. Inadvertently, my nursing career brought me full circle to my love of writing.

Anyone who nurses from a heart-centred place would agree that it is often impossible to leave experiences at work. The rates of divorce among nurses as a result of burnout was a topic joked about on my first day of school, with most of the instructors admitting they were remarried. I remember being struck by how accepting everyone seemed to be about the effect their career had on their personal lives, which I swore to myself to keep separate; After all, it was *my* husband that had taken me to my nursing school interview a few months earlier. I remember noticing him walking the grounds outside the office window at the point I was being offered the monumental choice to go to graduate school. I made the decision to go back to school from my head space, to be more successful and alleviate some of the financial responsibilities from my husband's shoulders. This was also a way to be further from financial dependency and female subservience.

The care I give is from a heart-centred place, but my decision to be a nurse was not from my soul's core. I spent the next two years of training struggling mentally and emotionally, as well as physically. I was suffering burnout between my life as a working mother and graduate student, my studies, my clinical placements, and any extra hours I could work to earn. Once I qualified, I was trying to navigate normal worries of the transition while dealing with the death and suffering of patients and colleagues, that I could never have imagined (especially after 9-11). I felt the return of the same soul disconnect as my time in *the wilderness*. I was angry and resentful, making sure my husband felt as miserable as I did by using our fleeting time and space together as a trauma dumping ground. I broke my promise to myself that I had made at the start, and nearly broke my marriage and once-thriving family life. I am now striving to regain my husband's trust and recreate a safe space where he can express his own vulnerability, an effort that could have been avoided entirely if I had just lived from my Truth. In order to repair my marriage and survive such an emotive career, I was determined to find peace once again, or at least a safe space for release.

From the first day of my nursing career, I began to journal as a way to decompress after most shifts and unpack what I was feeling at the time. Writing again was, and still is, cathartic and helps me to reframe the day's events. Keeping several journals, especially for my gratitude and soul work, helps me find crucial head and heart space connections. I spend the time just before each journaling session to take a sacred pause and, inadvertently, find the peace that comes from writing. Re-reading my entries helps me to identify themes that have broader meanings for living intentionally and improving work-life harmony.

In a recent journal entry, I noted the concept of providing a 'good death' in palliative nursing. This led me to reflect on how meaningful it is to a bereaved family to know that their loved one left this life peacefully. After repeating this statement to so many bereaved families, I came to understand this is why we, as humans, hope, seek, work, and pray for peace. For a 'good life' legacy, peace is the ultimate achievement, and it is experienced by each person uniquely. For me, I find peace in stillness, listening to my heart, and moving to the soul music that harmonises with the vibrations of my spirit. Whether it be in nature, pouring myself into a journaling session, or on a yoga mat in the middle of a crowded studio (like I found all those years ago). Taking sacred pauses are a necessary form of self-love and my answer to soul fatigue.

I first heard the terms soul minimalism and decision fatigue from spiritual genius, author, and podcaster, Emily P. Freeman, who asks the question about the decision to do *The Next Right Thing*, "Is it life-giving or is it life-draining?" I sat with my mouth wide open, shocked at how I could not have thought about such a basic consideration when struggling with soul fatigue. This was far better than a pro-con list. I began pondering this question every time I was faced with struggle or uncertainty. To return to love and connection with myself and others, my soul work, I began to use this question as a guidepost. At that time, I realised that this basic question was directly tied to my final project in nursing school, a holistic, person-centred coaching model.

I became so excited, visualising how I would combine this question and the model to create a hybrid way of mentoring others to combat fatigue and burnout. This can be applied to set soul goals in every area of life: career, relationships, personal development, finances, and even spirituality. I began to apply this hybrid model to my own life, taking sacred pauses to journal, tuning in and listening to the answers from my heart and head. Was it life-giving or life-draining? Were my decisions truly from my innermost spiritual self? My responses seemed to always be a simple yes or no. Another epiphany! Proving the results when I began to embody soul minimalism and find peace.

I liken soul minimalism to holistic decluttering, critiquing each area with love for life, working from the outside inwards. I looked at my mindset around personal and professional development, finance, relationships, and health -physical, emotional and mental. I separated everything into two categories. What was essential and what was non-essential? Everything that went into the non-essential category, I quit, discarded, or donated.

The most difficult area for this disposal was ending toxic relationships and constructing boundaries that I should have set long ago. By cleaving toxic relationships, it allows you the space to find your rightful tribe, those that are in the best alignment. My parents found their tribe and taught me how to forge a path led by heart and self-awareness. All the answers are within us if we can just quiet all of the other 'background noise'. Establishing internal and external boundaries meant a refusal to accept poor behaviour or blame from others. I am no one's drinking problem, door mat, or punching bag. This also meant recognising and stopping the unspoken expectations set upon us, or that we put onto others. I realised this process was helping me to clear out old conditioning, negative self-talk, and self-limiting beliefs. What was left in the essential category was prioritised. My family and self-care went to the top of that list.

After attending a mindfulness series, I read *The Warrior Wellbeing Toolkit* and joined The Warrior Academy, surrounded by other soul-guided women. I am infinitely grateful to Carol-Ann Reid. I attended my first ever vision board workshop, which revealed that I was meant to author my own story, suppressing suppression no longer. I began to pray again, I began to worship from my heart on my knees, embrace my inner child, to trust those 'gut instincts and the urge to purge. I gave myself permission to let go, or reversely, to accept and welcome in. When I listen to my heart in those sacred pauses, I can count on divine timing to bring me the solace I seek.

I am inspired by incredible warrior women (like my co-authors in this book), awakened by living from *their* soul centres to convert the energy of their pain into power. I resonate with the story of Cheryl Strayed in her book, *Wild*. On her mission of self-rediscovery, the author trekked along the Pacific Crest Trail (on my bucket list) and journaled reflections of her painful past and her future of uncertainty. Before leaving, she gathered only what she thought was essential, shedding more and more as she walked. Although she travelled an incredible distance, she could never shed her traumatic past, only the way she intentionally moved forward in her life. I loved her honesty about the unavoidable trauma and unselfish pleasure she bore to rewild and, ultimately, find her true self as a successful writer. I saw a lot of similarities in our stories. I too had to *rewild*. My ability to connect with my spiritual self was never lost.

Leaving my religion started a quest. Metaphorically speaking, I was asleep in my life, being born into and raised, through my formative years, in a fear-based, fundamentalist religion. In order to wake, I would have to navigate terrors both real and dreamt. I left my religion, and quickly awakened with my eyes wide shut, like the shock of jolting from a dream where you are falling and cannot scream. This decision set me on a trajectory in adulthood of breaking free, deconditioning, exploring and unlearning. I needed to know… who am I, really? Now I am equipped with the tools I never knew I always needed and possessed.

Part of finding my true self was stripping my soul, including the labels assigned by our roles, for example, avoiding the diminishing statement, *"I am just a… [insert: gender, job title, marital status, the Mum of…]"*. Labels evoke generalised, unspoken expectations of service value or monetary worth. Labels, like comparison, are works of the ego, as Eckart Tolle wrote in his book, A New Earth. We are entering a new era of awakening, where roles are shifting as fast mindsets. Awakened, I state, *"I* work as a nurse", rather than saying "I am a nurse", to avoid giving the impression that I fit into the inhumane rhetoric of a superhero or angel. There is so much more to me than titles, I am worthy of more than a label or the job I do.

If you find yourself wearing a label that is not in alignment with your spiritual self, you have the right and the power to shed it. It is okay to leave. You will be okay. You are still you. The awareness that I was no longer bound by the hourglass of an approaching Armageddon, no longer under the heavy cloud of judgement and inferiority, was the hardest work. There is no judgement, only negative self-talk and the unproductive criticism of others. Jealousy and comparison hold no power when we control the volume. If old, buried fears resurface, I cast them away with meditation and journaling. I no longer feel the need to wear my pain like a label or burn these accounts of my soul, but keep them as a reference of my evolution. I will continue this practice throughout the remainder of my life. The truth always sets you free, a bible verse I live by, one of many gifts from a past belief system that has both taken and given so much.

By all accounts, I do not believe *'light workers'* and empaths like myself ever 'get over' the traumas they experience but, rather, they convert the energy into love and send it back out to the universe. As the first law of thermodynamics states, "Energy is neither created nor destroyed, [...] it simply changes form". We channel the energy from our heart space to do the transformative work necessary to free our souls. I spent the first four decades of my life busy trying to find my true self through society's definition of knowledge and success. Imagine my surprise when I realised, all these years later, that my own true spirituality was always within if I just made the time for peace. My awakening arrived when I came to accept that I am not one thing, one label, but I am all things.

The time for life is now, so start living a soul-centred life as if *your* life depends on it because it does. The following tools have made my soul work, although hard at times, they are life-giving. You can adopt the practices that have worked for me, or find your own set of tools, but I call upon you to start your own soul work today.

Like the bible says, God is love, so go forth and love *yourself* and love *your* tribe with all of *your* heart and soul. Give yourself permission to **declutter your soul** and set soul goals to ensure you are surrounded by only what and whom is life-giving.

MY FIVE KEY TAKEAWAYS

1. Sing your heart out and dance like no one is watching to your own **warrior soul playlist**. Move to the music that speaks to your True spirit and tells your True story. Remember, you can still be a spiritualist and a headbanger! *You do You!*
2. Be mindful. **Take sacred pauses** to breathe, worship, pray, meditate, manifest, and vocalise mantras.
3. *Be In-lightened*! Use what evolves as your maps. Walk, run, and bathe in the wild to reconnect to your soul, immerse yourself in nature walks and earthing

rituals. Remember to speak life over yourself. Say, "*I can and I will!*"

4. Be a lifelong learner. Create and write to make things right. **Journal** every detail of your innermost feelings and thoughts that lead to awakening. Reflect on the lines of *your* page, themes that emerge and the snapshots of events, great and small; they all matter. Burn these if you must, but only on your terms.

5. Allow yourself the permission to walk your own path and speak your own Truth. Remember, ***it is okay to go****. You are enough. You've got this!*

My hope is that if you resonate with my story in some way, you will find my tools, or your own chosen ones, empowering and useful. You are an infinite source of life energy so *Shine on you Crazy Diamond* (Pink Floyd) *Across the Universe* (The Beatles). Jai Guru Deva (OM…) Glory to (you) the shining remover of darkness! I encourage you to carve out time for sacred pauses so you may find peace, so you may find happiness, and you may be free from suffering. Sending you infinite Blessings of Love and Light on your own awakening. Namaste.

ABOUT THE AUTHOR

SARAH RODGER JONES

Sarah Rodger Jones works as an Adult Nurse as part of her true calling to be a Light Worker. Sarah is developing her unique 1:1 coaching model based upon whole-life individualised soul-decluttering and minimalism, inspired by her own journey to clear the chaos and quiet the noise of busy modern-day life.

Having spent almost ten years achieving double degrees in Public Health and (Medical) Geography, Sarah was once described by a university professor as having 'an unquenchable thirst for knowledge'. Sarah became a reflexologist in 2012, taking cues from traditional practices, her own treatments for infertility, as well as biblical and ancient texts. Sarah applies this *'laying of hands* (-on)' approach to all of the holistic, person-centred care that she gives, believing that regular touch, especially hugging, is vital to human connection and healing.

In 2023, Sarah plans to resume teaching classes in mindfulness, yoga, and dance, that will help inspire people to move towards understanding their own life rhythms and soul playlist.

After marrying her soulmate 13 years ago, together they manifested their dream farmhouse and garden, where they raise their young son with an 'old soul', and their four-legged fur baby. Being curators of its' antiquity, their safe haven in North Wales is a perfect place for taking essential 'sacred' pauses. Sarah is a lover of all things *spiritual* and harnesses her beliefs and faith through prayer and meditation, crystals, women's circles, and moon ceremonies. Sarah also attends a traditional Christian church, where she will, finally, be submerged in water for baptism this year.

Sarah is available for 1:1 sessions to empower and mentor clients to navigate their own self-directed path to '*Inlightenment*'.

To work or connect with Sarah, visit:

Facebook.com/balancedreflexionswellbeing

Email: sarahprodger@gmail.com

facebook.com/sarahrodgerjones
instagram.com/sarahrodgerjones

10

AWAKENING MY PERSONAL GROWTH AND DEVELOPMENT

SHARON WATERMAN

> "There comes a point where we need to stop pulling people out of the river. We need to go upstream and find out why they are falling in."
>
> — DESMOND TUTU

I didn't see the signs before it was too late. I needed pulling out of the river. I'm not sure when I fell in. Should I have seen the signs that it was coming? With hindsight, if I hadn't fallen in, battling with the demons of my self-doubt, becoming a shadow of my former self, I would not have had the awakening I did.

How did it happen? Personal trauma due to bereavement, diagnosis of a rare medical condition, and some painful experiences in the workplace over a period of time certainly contributed to a near breakdown. I didn't see it coming.

I was coping, then I wasn't. It all got too much and I had to admit that for the first time in my life, this was not something I could fix on my own.

As an educator with several decades of experience, I was used to pulling others out of the river. That's what we do in education, we find issues and fix them. I was strong, resilient, a strategic thinker and problem solver. I was a coach. I had received counselling in the past, but it wasn't until I began working with a coach myself that the real awakening began, when I was actually pulled out of the river.

My journey of awakening has been transformational, and I'm proud to say that I am now so much more aligned with my personal values, and the most assured, confident, and fulfilled version of me I've ever been. The bold steps I took have given me flexibility, freedom and variety in my work, and I am definitely more present for my family.

Consciously making time for personal growth and development is now important to me as I didn't do this for the whole of my career. Reading, exercise, meditation, and journaling are staple features of my day, which has ignited my passion for coaching and my mission to help others to become the best version of themselves. I dedicate my work to light the way for others who, like me, may have painted on the corporate mask. I work to raise an awareness that spending time on personal growth and development is just as, if not more important, than professional development. I consider this going upstream to stop people falling in the river.

It took a long time for me to realise the change happening to me was potentially a spiritual one - that there were higher forces or the universe at play. This wasn't something I had previously considered. I felt I was a lucky person when good things happened, I now have a different level of understanding.

Looking back, I previously had a spiritual connection. As a child, every Sunday my younger sister and I went to Sunday school at the local Salvation Army, and we were educated to hold firm beliefs in Christianity. We weren't particularly religious but I recognise now that the connection with a higher being or the universe was there, I had just forgotten, or parked, a spiritual connection at that point in my life, which leads me to recall other aspects of my upbringing that may have shaped how I approached my career.

I grew up on a council estate on the outskirts of Nottingham. I was the first in my family to go to university. I don't think that many people from my school went to university, I certainly don't judge them for this as the friends I grew up with are successful and content, we just took a different path.

I believe all children deserve a champion and for me, this was a PE teacher. She spotted potential and helped raise my aspirations, as I could have quite easily have gone down a different path. I had a good upbringing, but my parents weren't aspirational - very few people were back then, and this is not a "woe is me" story. What drove me back then was my dream of becoming a teacher, so I focused on what I

AWAKENING MY PERSONAL GROWTH AND DEVELOPMENT

needed to do to get me there; the qualifications I needed to get me to the next stage.

This wasn't straightforward, as I left school at 16 with three GCSEs, barely enough to get into the sixth form college I wanted to join. Determined and driven by my dream, I did it - and that is where the focus on my career began, leaving no time for my personal development and growth.

Looking back at my younger self, the experiences and drive I had most definitely shaped a belief in me that I would always have something to prove, that the kid from the council estate, who left school with three GCSEs could do it, could become educated to degree level. I carried a demon that someone could always come and take that away from me, because I didn't deserve it. Many of you will recognise this as imposter syndrome.

If I could talk to my 19-year-old self as I left home to go to university to train to be a teacher, I would tell her 'The only person you have to prove something to is yourself'... I am not sure I would have listened though.

The imposter syndrome, present throughout my career, drove a focus on professional development. This was, and still is, a responsibility of all teachers. It is written in the 'Teachers' Standards', which define the level of practice expected of teachers and is used to assess performance.

Teaching is often referred to as a vocation, a career that requires dedication. Many teachers share that their inspiration to become a teacher was, in fact, a teacher; someone who made a difference to them. Remember my PE teacher? She was that inspiration to me. That's what teachers want to do, make a difference. In order to make a difference, we have to evolve and keep on top of developments, changes, and so many initiatives and strategies. To be the best teacher, you place your focus on professional development, to make a difference. I like to think that a few of my former pupils and colleagues would say that I did.

The focus for me was performing well in my job, taking a course or enrolling on a qualification to improve or progress to the next promotion, and this worked. I had a great career. Every new role I took was the next dream job. I relished every new challenge and opportunity to extend myself and develop as a leader. I worked with amazing colleagues, was given so many opportunities to progress and learn from inspirational leaders. However, it would be wrong not to acknowledge that not all the experiences I had during my career were positive. With so much pressure and expectation to deliver, it's easy to create a culture lacking in psychological safety.

I have either witnessed or experienced some unpleasant moments during my career - fortunately very few involving children. It saddens me to say workplace bullying exists; there are leaders who lack emotional intelligence and are focused on their own agenda, driven to get what they want, often casting colleagues aside once they have served their purpose. This might get results but it has a cost, often relationships. It leaves colleagues feeling disillusioned, disengaged, and disconnected with the values that brought them into the profession in the first place.

Moving forward, I focussed on the positives in my career: opportunities, motivational leaders providing pupils and colleagues with inspirational and transformational experiences. I was learning about education and leadership, but not learning about myself.

Was I aware of this at the time? Absolutely not. Everything was going well. Looking back, it was my choice, but I didn't have a good work life balance. My career was so important, I was putting in the hours to prove that I was working hard. I once heard myself referred to by a colleague as a 'machine', and took this as a compliment.

I was aware of my skillset; I was approachable, a good organiser and problem solver, turning strategy into implementation. Very little fazed me. I was a good teacher and, according to Ofsted, an outstanding leader. I developed colleagues professionally, trained the future generation of teachers, and loved what I was doing.

Outside of work I had very few responsibilities, thanks to a good home life and supportive partner, who eventually became my husband. I had, and still have, great friends who have always been there for me. I escaped the stresses of work playing netball and golf, travelling to beautiful places in the world. I was making my family proud and I was proving myself.

I didn't see that this might be storing something up that might unravel in my future. Only when we go back and connect the dots can we see where this might have been heading. Knowing this now, I can hopefully predict and prevent ever falling in the river again.

The emerging theme is neglect of myself; specifically of my personal growth and development. Playing sport, having great holidays, and friends, helped to distract and relax me, but when I needed something more, when I faced personal trauma and became ill, having to change my whole life focus, I simply didn't know how. Lacking the skillset, I developed a shield, a way of coping some might refer to as a corporate mask - presenting that everything was OK but inside, something was spiralling. My imposter syndrome was the strongest it had ever been. I lacked self-belief, lost sight of my values, and couldn't see a way out. I couldn't possibly walk away from my career; everything I worked for would be lost, I would be seen as a failure. I had been in education since the age of five, an employee since the age of 22. I didn't know anything else; I would be letting everyone down.

It might sound strange, but working through this with a coach, I now believe my higher self, or the universe, was working to create this version of me, the shadow of my former self, because something needed to change, I needed an awakening.

I have recently qualified as a Neuro Linguistic Programming (NLP) Coach, so I am fully aware that our bodies and minds have an amazing capacity to heal and build resilience to counteract the vulnerabilities our beliefs predispose us to. We can be reprogrammed. Before I share how this took place, it is time to revisit some of the life-changing events which contributed to me falling in the river and the decisions I had to take to heal.

As a child of elderly parents - mum was 40 when she had me in 1969 - I had an awareness of loss. I lost my grandparents by my early teens and in my subconscious, I always knew that my parents wouldn't be around forever. This proved to be the case. By the time I was 43, both of my parents had died and I had also lost a close friend to Leukaemia when we were only 26.

In 2016, something I never imagined would happen, did - the loss of my younger sister to breast cancer. She was only 43. It all happened so quickly, within 11 months of her initial diagnosis she was gone. I felt completely out of control. My skillset included problem solver, but this was something I couldn't fix. I couldn't fix her. We had very little time to prepare for it and had an added complication, she was a single parent of a five-year-old boy. Living over 170 miles away, I suffered the guilt of not being there as often as I could, grateful that she had close friends who did so much for her, which wasn't easy for them as they had their own families.

Looking back, I didn't allow myself to grieve, I wasn't intuitive enough; I went into operational, organisational mode. I had a problem and this one I could fix. Firstly, the funeral, then her estate, the legalities of a Care Arrangement Order, and moving my nephew 170 miles south to begin the next chapter of his life.

I wasn't maternal. We weren't parents, children weren't part of our plan. Our lives would be completely different and we adjusted with help from family, friends, and his school. We drew on all the support and resources we could, seemingly making it up as we went along. I did seek the help of a counsellor who helped me to understand and process the waves of grief that would hit me, and that sharing, talking, and crying - which I did, especially with my nephew - would help me to heal. But while all of my focus was on him, I failed to realise I was neglecting myself.

My nephew settled in well, showing amazing resilience for one so young, and I threw myself into our new life. Thanks to the support of my husband, family, friends, work, and a lovely childminder, I could maintain the high professional expectations I had of myself. We needed to make it work, I had to prove that I could make it work both professionally and at home. It did, and I was flying high in my career. I had another dream job, which gave me a bit more flexibility, and thought that I would be doing this until I retired.

A few years later, I suffered another loss; my elder brother - my hero, again, to cancer and, like my sister, it happened so quickly. I went back to the counsellor and a few sessions helped, but my self-talk was telling me 'You've got this', 'you know how to deal with grief', knowing that I needed to support my nephew, who was experiencing another significant loss at the age of eight.

Work was supportive and I continued to love my dream job, but something changed. I don't know when, why, or how it started, but I began to think differently, feel differently. The imposter syndrome was starting to raise its head. The self-doubts and paranoia crept back in and I felt I needed to prove myself in everything I did.

I started to recognise a few symptoms that were becoming more regular; when standing, I started to feel shaking and tremors in my legs. Once, when standing on a station platform, I remember feeling that my legs might give way and panicking as I couldn't find anywhere to sit. I started to notice a pattern, linked to times of stress and pressure, not always limited to the working day but more often than not. They became more frequent, even at periods of rest, in bed, when trying to go to sleep.

I didn't know how to deal with this but I was determined it wasn't going to affect my work. I didn't want to show signs of weakness and certainly didn't want to be judged. Again, this was something that I couldn't control, so sought the help of a neurologist who diagnosed a rare medical condition, thankfully not degenerative, but one that I would need medication and to develop coping strategies for, for the rest of my life.

This all took place during the pandemic, the period of lockdown which I also think, like so many others, changed me.

Working online from home made everything different, even though education seemed to adapt and carry on. Some people find change difficult, I always seemed to embrace it as an opportunity, especially when it is out of my control. I considered myself to be resilient, having introduced programmes to equip pupils and teachers with the skills of resilience through an amazing charity called Bounce Forward, that I am still connected with.

I was a resilient person, but things were changing that I had no control over. Things at work, plus my physical and mental health, gave me an overwhelming sense these factors were working against me to drag me down, and no matter how hard I tried, I couldn't scramble up the river bank; I let go and fell in. I needed to take some bold steps to bring about change. I knew that I still had so much to offer education but it was time for a change in direction, a new career.

The decision to leave an executive career behind was made and while I could take my time to consider a new direction, it wasn't the awakening I anticipated it would be. It actually made me feel more vulnerable. I wasn't out of the river yet.

Recognising that I couldn't fix this on my own, I sought help, first from a counsellor who worked on mindfulness strategies, distress tolerance, and Eye Movement Desensitisation and Reprocessing - a psychotherapy treatment for the recovery of trauma. I don't know how much this helped, but it did open my eyes to alternative approaches.

I started engaging in a few other programmes that would help me heal, including work on mindset, developing greater resilience, and gaining a professional coaching qualification, not realising at the time that this was personal development; I thought it another professional qualification. These programmes ignited a passion, initially in coaching, that had lain dormant for some time. They also helped me to see how I could use these techniques to help others.

I enrolled on a mindset mastermind programme, working with an amazing coach. I enjoyed it so much, and felt so aligned with the way the programme was shaping my thinking about my own growth and development. I felt connected and didn't want the relationship to end. I saw a path to help me heal and move forwards through individual coaching. I came to the realisation that even coaches need a coach.

I was working with a coach, not only to pull me out of the river and heal, but also to navigate my future career so that I would never be in the same position again. We both knew I still had so much to offer, but I would be doing so with a greater spirituality, connecting with what the universe has to offer in terms of help and guidance.

In one of the latter sessions, a question was posed, which I then realised was my initial awakening about how I fell into the river. She asked if I had ever considered that my higher self, or the universe, had made me ill, and brought all of the painful experiences together to protect my future self?

This question opened my mind and raised an awareness to something that I didn't recall I had considered before. It awakened a greater sense of awareness that what I had always attributed to good luck was, in fact, my higher self, or the universe, manifesting things to happen, and that this was the path meant for me.

I needed more proof that this could be the case. My bookshelf started to look very different; the leadership books were replaced with literature about personal development, growth, and wisdom. It was in one of those books that I found another awakening, The Four Agreements by Don Miguel Ruiz. The Four Agreements are: Be Impeccable with Your Word, Don't Take Anything Personally, Don't Make Assumptions, Always Do Your Best. These revealed to me how limiting beliefs can prevent us from being happy. I had been provided with a code of conduct I could hold myself accountable to. This simple framework has transformed my life to experience the new found freedom my career is now giving me.

A new version of me was starting to emerge; my health was much improved, the shakes and tremors were less frequent, and I was able to gradually reduce medication. Now I was focusing on my personal growth and development, starting to shape the direction of my new career. I realised that the balance I thought I was looking for to show me I was healing was a becoming a barrier to moving forward. I assumed that I would achieve a better work-life balance. I kept telling myself I wasn't getting the balance right between family, my new passion for personal growth, and the new career I was creating. It wasn't actually balance that I was seeking, but a sense of greater harmony. Different parts of our lives mean more at different times, and you don't need to measure how much time they have in a day.

This realisation about harmony wasn't down to one lightbulb moment, more of a culmination of a few over time, coupled with an emerging sense that I was starting to become the best version of myself.

My new career is ever evolving, regularly taking me outside of the comfort zone that may have previously restricted my growth. My values are more aligned with what I do and as a result, I am more confident. I am my own boss, working hard for the people I coach and the organisations I work for. I have a fulfilling sense of pride in what I do, rather than proving to others that I can do what I am being asked to do.

It has taken time to shake off my imposter syndrome as I lost a great deal of confidence and questioned whether I really had anything to offer. The feedback I am given is very positive, which gives me huge satisfaction, building a reputation in a very competitive market. I set my own expectations and goals, and decide who I work with and when I do it, which is very liberating.

Having had a long career in education, I had built strong networks and you get to know who you can rely on and ask for help when faced with challenges, as I did. Previously, I would have attributed this to luck but these days, being more intuitive, I realise that this is the path I am supposed to follow. The networks and friends who are still with me are so because we have built relationships based on mutual trust, understanding, and a willingness to go above and beyond for others when they need it. We may be at different stages of the journey and have different career paths, but there is a support network we can all call on.

What I have learned was lacking throughout my career was the need to focus on my personal growth and development. It is now more important to me than my professional development and I build this into my daily routines. It hasn't been easy, after being institutionalised by a system that gives great opportunities and a sense that you are making a difference in so many lives, but can also drive you to the edge of burnout due to workload and fear of judgement when you should be asking for help.

I also needed to clarify what personal growth actually meant to me and accept that the awakening I had was normal and not something to hide from others. I found this through reading, mindset programmes, and joining an online membership group that provided me with a support network of like-minded warriors outside of education. My personal growth involves mindfulness, recording the intentions for my continued growth in a journal, creating time in a busy schedule for me and not feeling a failure if I don't always stick to the routines I have set. I am definitely more present in my life.

Interestingly, for someone so focused and self-directed, I have had to reset my thinking and organise my time differently, possibly due to being institutionalised. At first, I felt so disorganised on a Monday, I had shed the sleepless Sunday nights which were around for the majority of my career, but if I wasn't contracted to be somewhere on a Monday, I felt that I wasn't effective, I didn't achieve what I wanted to do in the time I had allocated.

A simple Neuro-Linguistic Programming anchoring technique to help with procrastination helped make me more motivated. Revisiting one of The Four Agreements, To Always Do Your Best, I acknowledged that my best is different at various times of the day and week, but recognising that I was still doing my best certainly helped to achieve the harmony I was seeking.

I began to schedule work and personal growth time during the day, including joining a weekly live group I am a member of, whenever I am able to. My Monday mindset is now aligned with my values, and the flexible routines I have created ensure I end the day feeling I have achieved a greater sense of harmony, which I once referred to as balance.

I show daily gratitude in my journal for the flexibility and freedom I have been given to create a new direction for my career as my confidence, focus and self-direction are now giving me the power to create wonderful opportunities, both in my work and my life. In my daily journal, I commit to adopting The Four Agreements in my life, I show gratitude for the people and opportunities I have had, some would seem so small and insignificant to others, but this is my space to express and set the intention for how I will make the day great. When I first started to journal, I used to list 'what will make the day great' but realised that this linked the outcome to an external source, so I switched it to something I had control over.

I also recognise my growth as a parent. I am more present for my family and we are closer as a result. I still don't consider myself to be a mother, that would betray my sister as I am not replacing her, but I do have a strong bond with my nephew and I know I am doing what my sister wanted. She would be so proud of who her son is becoming. Due to my intuitive awakening, it has made me realise that sometimes the toughest times give us the greatest gifts.

The skillset I acquired throughout my career I thought was only applicable to education. In the early days, my self-talk told me that education was the only institution I knew, how could I possibly have anything to offer other sectors? Considering my experiences, which could have happened in any industry, I now realise that this is far from my initial perceptions. When training to be a coach, I thought that I would only be accepted by educationalists, and the Neuro Linguistic Programming I was learning would only be used in education, but this has opened so many opportunities to work with individuals and teams in a variety of settings.

The strength I have gained from my journey, driving me to focus on my personal growth and development, is something I share with others, and do so from my personal experience of what could happen if you don't make this a priority. There is definitely a change in the approaches to wellbeing of staff in the workplace and as a result, we are becoming more intuitively able to recognise our needs, but do we always listen to what our bodies and minds are saying? Or do we hide behind the corporate mask, fearing judgement?

I now channel my experience, qualifications, and wisdom to support others to avoid the need to reach for the corporate mask, as I did, but to use their intuition, recognising the benefits that finding time for their personal development will bring all aspects of work and life.

There are so many teachers and leaders leaving education due to a variety of reasons, including stress, and I am sure this is not uncommon in other industries. Going back to the river analogy, let's consider what we can do upstream to stop people from falling in.

What if individuals considering leaving the career they have worked so hard for, were given time to focus on personal development, and had a psychologically safe support structure, without fear of judgement? Would they still fall in the river?

I have had the pleasure of working with clients to explore the reasons they wanted to either leave their current job or consider a change in profession. They didn't fall in the river but without intervention, they may well have. Exploring the key driver for the desired change has so often led to a wider reflection of the challenges they face in their current role, for some, it has resulted in a promotion in another organisation, or revisiting their values and beliefs about why they were looking for a change. For some, this has been their own awakening.

These clients were doing exactly what I should have done earlier in my career, they were investing in themselves. They sought out a coach to open their mind to new opportunities and possibilities to help them on their own journey to an awakening.

It was through a mutual friend, but also, I believe the universe, that connected me to the coach I began working with, she has helped me rethink my future career, awakening a connection that had lain dormant since before my career in education began. Looking back to that painful time, I had already started to focus on my personal growth, through the coaching qualification I funded prior to me making the huge decision to leave my executive career in education.

I was making time for myself, which ignited the passion I had for coaching and I saw a way that I could fulfil my ambition to help others become the best version of themselves.

My hope for you is that whatever your chosen career or situation you find yourself in, you will achieve a greater awareness that your own personal growth and development must be, at the very least, of equal focus to your professional development.

When you are able to recognise the benefits of this awareness, you will be able to identify what this means for you and choose what will work for you. For me, it was coaching, working on mindset, meditation, using a journal to state my intentions, reading for my own personal growth and development, engaging in networks that gave me a safe space, free from judgement, and finally, regularly checking in with myself so that I am able to recognise if the harmony or balance that keeps me on track is becoming unstable.

My career is more fulfilling as I can draw on the challenges, experiences, and learnings during my awakening journey which has been part of my own personal growth and development. By using my skills to coach others, creating a psychologically safe social media network of educationalists who can seek guidance and support, without judgment, and helping them to focus on personal as well as professional growth, I achieve a greater sense of personal satisfaction and fulfilment.

You have nothing to lose by committing and allocating time to this so that you never have to wear the corporate mask or you never find yourself in need of being pulled out of the river.

FIVE KEY TAKEAWAYS:

1. The first step is to use your intuition; acknowledge that personal growth and development are just as important as professional development.
2. Once this has been achieved, you need to be able to identify what personal growth and development mean to you, we are all unique.
3. Set the intention for how you will commit to your personal growth and development, what are you going to do?
4. Don't be afraid to seek the help and assistance of others; a coach, friend, colleague, or a social network group of like-minded individuals where you can feel psychologically safe, as they will help you on your journey and keep you accountable.
5. Use your intuition to help others; the above may stop you from falling into the river, but there are others we can all still look out for.

ABOUT THE AUTHOR

SHARON WATERMAN

Sharon is a passionate NLP coach, consultant, and educator. As Managing Director of her own coaching and consultancy business, she draws on nearly 30 years' experience in education, where she successfully led and unlocked potential in thousands of teachers, leaders, and associate staff, to now achieving her ambition of helping many others to become the best version of themselves.

Before starting her own business, Sharon's successful career in education saw her appointed to numerous senior leader and executive positions in schools across the country. A strong feature of Sharon's leadership was to focus on the development of others but due to her awakening, she now focuses equally on personal growth as well as professional development.

A Trustee for the charity, Bounce Forward, since it began, Sharon has been instrumental in the promotion of the Healthy Minds Programme in schools, which provides training for teachers in the delivery of psychological fitness and resilience for children.

When Sharon lost her sister to cancer in 2016, she and her husband began a new and exciting journey, becoming parents to her young nephew. In her spare time, Sharon can be found on the golf course, cycling around the Kent countryside, or working out at the gym.

Sharon is available for individual and team coaching, training, and education consultancy. She is the expert host of her community, 'Everything Education', which provides a psychologically safe space for educators to network, share ideas, and ask advice.

You can reach Sharon at:

Email: Sharon@watermancc.com

Website: https://watermancoachingandconsultancy.com

Everything Education Facebook Group:

www.facebook.com/groups/5184428638302441

f facebook.com/watermancoaching

○ instagram.com/watermancoaching

in linkedin.com/in/sharon-waterman-ba7166a4

Printed in Great Britain
by Amazon